CW01499805

Some names, location   have
been changed to protect the identities of the individuals
who were either witnesses to or victims of these
phenomena.

Evil Unleashed

True Tales of Spells Gone to Hell and Other Occult Disasters

John Harker

Evil Unleashed: True Tales of Spells Gone to Hell and Other Occult Disasters

ISBN-13: 978-1540363725
ISBN-10: 1540363724

Photo Credits:

In memory of Father Gabriele Amorth, who battled the forces of evil for more than 30 years as Rome's chief exorcist.

(May 1, 1925 - September 16, 2016)

Table of Contents

Introduction

Interest in the occult is booming. Even the most casual perusal of books, television shows, movies, music, and websites will uncover an amazing amount of occult material available for young and old alike. Many of the offerings are subtle in their presentation, with titles and descriptions that include highbrow words such as esotericism, metaphysics, quantum mysticism, Rosicrucianism, and Theosophy. Nothing scary-sounding there. They could be courses offered in a college catalog. In fact, they probably are.

On the other end of the spectrum are the scarier-sounding, hard-core occult topics such as witchcraft, sorcery, black magic, and Satanism. In between are all manner of "tamer" occult diversions such as astrology, white magic, fortune telling, divination, and necromancy (communicating with the dead).

The one thing all these subjects, and many more, have in common—and what makes them appealing to so many people—is the promise of hidden knowledge. Who doesn't want to unlock the secrets of the Universe? Who wouldn't like to know how to conjure up a better job, more money, a true love? Who wouldn't want to talk to their dear deceased Aunt Flo and discover what it's like on the Other Side?

Apparently, quite a few. In recent years, there has been a tremendous uptick in the number of people participating in occult activities. A number of factors are responsible, including a falling away from traditional religion, the need to fill a spiritual void with something new and exciting, and easy access to "how to" manuals. (Need a love spell? Just ask Google.)

While all of this is great news for freelance witches, television mediums, online fortune tellers, and other occult vendors, it has become disastrous for many individuals who have left themselves open to evil forces by immersing themselves—or merely dabbling—in the dark arts.

The occult is dangerous. Ouija boards, séances, mediums, Tarot cards, spells, curses, satanic rites and rituals—all of these things facilitate the crossing over of evil spirits into the human realm, your realm. And once you attract malevolent spirits into your life, they're really, *really* hard to get rid of. Hanging out with you and making your life miserable is a whole lot more fun than going back to where they came from. (One exorcist related that a demon he was expelling from a woman begged to stay because he feared punishment from "the master" for failing.)

Sometimes it's possible for a person to get rid of the trouble on their own, depending on the level and intensity of the spirit activity. This might involve burning all occult paraphernalia, reciting prayers of deliverance, and/or making a major lifestyle change like moving to a new location. Other times the help of a professional—a clergyman, exorcist, demonologist, or gifted paranormal expert—is needed to banish the tormentors. In all instances, the individual *must* be predisposed to renouncing the occult activity.

If ever there was an example of a slippery slope, it is in the realm of the occult. A person (we'll call her Amy) starts with, let's say, having her palm read. The next day Amy runs into an old boyfriend, just like the palm reader said. (Well, she said a "surprise" would come her way. Close enough.) Amy's appetite is whetted. She picks up a book on ceremonial magic and performs a candle spell for good fortune. Later, she finds a five-dollar bill on the floor of her car. Woo-hoo! She must be on to something! The next week while shopping at Toys "R" Us for her niece's birthday, she spots a Ouija board nestled among the other board games. What the heck? She buys Hungry Hippos for her niece and the Ouija for herself. That night Amy and her girlfriend attempt to raise a spirit. They get one! It's an acquaintance from high school who died his senior year in a car crash. At least, it says that's who it is. It wouldn't lie about something like that, would it?

Of course it would. And now Amy has just opened herself up to an unsavory spirit who seized an opportunity to intervene in Amy's world. The spirit might have first noticed Amy at the palm reader's shop and decided to go home with her. It could have been invoked during the candle ritual. Or it could have simply been the first to answer Amy's unwitting "come on in, whoever!" call that the Ouija board so notoriously facilitates.

Amy is not a hard-core devil worshipper, but she still has opened herself up to a whole lot of trouble. Though our example here is fictional, the ugly reality is that any involvement with the occult, even passive participation, will more often than not take a serious toll on one's physical, mental, and spiritual health. Walter Cascioli, spokesman for the Italy-based International Association of Exorcists (IAE), warns that the ramifications of occult activity include anxiety, panic attacks, nightmares, acts of self-harm, and constant thoughts of death, to name a few. In severe cases, occult activity can lead to demonic possession. "The consequences are always disastrous," he says.

Sadly, warnings like these are falling on deaf ears. The global surge in popularity of the occult has led to a not-surprising correlative increase in the demand for exorcisms. According to the IAE, the number of requests for exorcisms in Italy alone was a staggering 500,000 in 2015. In the U.S., the number of exorcists appointed by bishops has risen from 12 to 50 in the last 20 years to handle the number of requests. Unfortunately, there are still not enough trained exorcists available to handle the load. Father Gary Thomas, an exorcist in the diocese of San José, knows this firsthand. "I am a full-time pastor and this is a very intense ministry. Almost every free night that I have is taken up with exorcisms," he says.

The Reverend Vincent Lambert is an exorcist in the diocese of Indianapolis. He states that while the request for exorcisms has skyrocketed, only one out of every 5,000 requests is a case of full-blown demonic possession. Nonetheless, he has conducted countless exorcisms related to demonic obsession, vexation, and infestation. "From a faith perspective it may seem like the devil has upped his game, so to speak. I don't think the devil has upped his game, but more people are inclined to play that game," says Lambert.

While some occult practitioners, like "white witches," do not usually intend for anything bad to happen when they practice their craft, others—black witches, sorcerers, Satanists—most definitely do. Using profane rituals, they are able to summon specific demons and command them to do their bidding. Their common objectives are to attain money, prestige, personal power, sexual conquests, and the ruin of their adversaries. They are often successful. But at a steep price.

Renowned demonologist Ed Warren put it like this: "The demonic is a loan shark, and it not only collects before you're ready, it wants double in return for what it gives. Ultimately it wants the soul." Involvement in the occult always backfires, in one form or another. It can be quick or it can take a number of years. But be assured that the spirits you bargain with will never let you off the hook.

Demonology expert and exorcist Father José Fortea of Madrid, Spain, echoes this warning in a discussion about curses: "Many people ask if curses are truly effective. Well, the first thing that has to be said is that whoever does the curse—as well as the person who may have asked for the curse to be done—will be the first one affected by the demonic. Without a doubt, they will suffer some type of demonic influence, possession, or sickness. The evil they wish on another will come back to them. A demon is never invoked in vain."

The stories that follow are true, though some identifying details have been changed to protect the privacy of the individuals involved. They all illustrate, each in their own way, the dangers of partaking in occult activities or, in the case of at least one unfortunate person, being a target of occult bedevilment. Some of the consequences are more severe than others. Some of the cases are resolved more easily than others. Some of the cases are not resolved at all.

This is the nature of occult entanglement. It's messy, murky, and malignant. The evil it invokes is like a vicious form of cancer: it's hard to get rid of completely, and often it comes back, more virulent than before. Only in this case, it's not just the body that's being assaulted, but also the soul.

* * *

"If you want to figure out the spirit world while you're alive, then beware—the deeper you get into it, the deeper they may want you, and the more powerful the pull is to find the answers."

– **Zak Bagans, paranormal investigator and host of**
Ghost Adventures

1

The Beast

There is arguably no other figure in recent history who influenced the development of the modern-day occult movement as much as Aleister Crowley. He is largely credited with having popularized "magick" in England and bringing it to America in the early 20th century. His famous one-line moral code, "Do What Thou Wilt," has become the central creed of the neo-pagan, Wicca, and witchcraft communities. And his esoteric spiritual teachings have influenced a long line of occult and cult leaders, including Gerald Gardner, founder of Gardnerian Wicca, L. Ron Hubbard, founder of Scientology, and Anton LaVey and Michael Aquino, leaders in religious Satanism.

The following examination of Aleister Crowley's life and times is intended to show how a life dedicated to the occult can end in disaster and ruin for one and for many. Though admirers will argue that Crowley was a mystical genius and spiritual prophet, most people, it is hoped, will view him as the creature he truly was: a pathetic, perverted, repugnant beast.

* * *

Aleister Crowley (1875-1947) was the most notorious occultist of his time. Given the title "The Wickedest Man Alive" by the tabloid press, and calling himself "The Great

Beast 666," Crowley strove mightily to live up to his reputation through his writings and teachings, his outlandish behavior, and his hedonistic lifestyle. In fact, no one thought more of Aleister Crowley than Aleister himself.

Raised by strict fundamentalist parents in an English household, Crowley grew to despise Christianity at an early age. Rebellious and ill-tempered, his parents often dubbed him "the Beast of Revelation." When his father died of cancer in 1887, the young Crowley was left with ample opportunity and a good chunk of the family fortune to indulge his earthly passions and pursuits, of which there were many. Chess, poetry, and mountain climbing were among his tamer interests. But it was sex and drugs that preoccupied most of Crowley's time and energy, and which got him into the most trouble, both in and out of school.

Crowley may have been undisciplined but he was no dolt. He entered Cambridge in 1895, where he formally changed his name from Edward (his birth name) to Aleister. During his time there, he studied philosophy and English literature and began his own self-guided study of the occult. A popular story from that time describes how Crowley made an effigy of a professor who had scolded him and used it in a black magic ritual performed with several classmates. During the ritual, Crowley stabbed the effigy's leg with a needle. The next day the professor fell down a flight of steps and broke his leg.

After Cambridge, Crowley traveled around Europe and pursued in earnest his interest in mountain climbing. He proved quite adept at the sport, and in 1902, he attempted to climb K2, the second-highest peak in the world. He got as far up as 20,000 feet before being forced to turn back by bad weather. Over the years, Crowley's reputation among other climbers was tarnished by repeated reports of his bad behavior toward his climbing partners, which went as far as causing them bodily harm and even, it was rumored, death on one or more occasions.

Crowley in a Hermetic Order of the Golden Dawn ritual as resurrected Osiris

In 1898, Crowley joined the burgeoning British occult group the Hermetic Order of the Golden Dawn. The HOGD was dedicated to the study of ceremonial magic, metaphysics, and alchemy. Crowley proved to be a quick study and rose quickly through the ranks on his way to the society's inner circle. But even an occult group open to "enlightened" and "progressive" thinking could not entertain Crowley's excessive sexual antics and drug use, and he eventually became isolated from the group.

In 1899, Crowley bought an eighteenth-century mansion on the southeastern shore of Loch Ness in Scotland. The residence was called Boleskine House and it quickly became the source of dark rumors and whispered warnings among the local residents. Already saddled with an auspicious beginning—the mansion had supposedly been built on the site of a church where the congregation had once burned to death in a fire while at Mass—Boleskine captured Crowley's fancy as a "Magical East" that was perfect in location and design for performing intense magical rituals.

In particular, Crowley was obsessed with a complicated, six-month ritual described in the *Book of the Sacred Magic of Abramelin* that had as its end goal contact with one's Guardian Angel, who would then supposedly impart magical wisdom to its invoker. But first, the spell-master had to invoke what Crowley called the Lords of Darkness and compel them via the ritual to serve the forces of Good, an action that needed to be undertaken with great care, as these dark forces were not amenable to making such a change willingly.

Crowley began the ritual but was called away in the middle of it by a Golden Dawn leadership crisis in Paris. Before he left, Crowley noted in his diary that the rite seemed to be having strange effects on his property, and feared it could be the doings of the "Abramelin devils." His housemaid abruptly quit and another worker went insane. The local butcher accidentally cut off his hand after reading a meat order from Crowley that on its back were scrawled the names of demons. After Crowley left, rumors of strange goings-on intensified. Large black clouds seemed to endlessly hover over the estate. People mysteriously died or disappeared. Soon it was being reported that the uncompleted ceremony had resulted in demons arising and running amok in the community. Some even claimed the unfinished rite was responsible for a huge, monstrous entity in Loch Ness.

Over the next several years, Crowley journeyed around the world, climbing mountains and studying various forms of mysticism that included Hinduism and Buddhism. In 1904 he married Rose Kelly, the sister of an artist friend, Gerald Kelly. The two honeymooned in Egypt, where Crowley claimed to have contacted the Egyptian god Horus through his messenger, a supernatural entity named Aiwass. Aiwass supposedly dictated a religious codex to Crowley entitled *The Book of the Law*. It was to be the manifesto for a new post-Christian age "religion" which Crowley would lead as its chief prophet. Crowley called this new philosophy system Thelema and added more volumes to it over time. *The Book of the Law* remained the cornerstone of Thelema, instructing its followers to discover their destined paths in life through the practice of magick and to adhere to the central tenet of "Do what thou wilt."

In 1905, Rose gave birth to Crowley's daughter Lilith. While Rose spent most of her time caring for the infant, and becoming increasingly dependent on alcohol, Crowley continued to indulge his "Do what thou wilt" axiom. He flaunted his bacchanalian lifestyle with a never-ending stream of mistresses and prostitutes—both male and female—ritualized orgies, heavy cocaine and heroin use, pornographic writings, and bizarre self-proclaimed titles such as "Baphomet," "Ipsissimus," "The Great Beast 666," and anything else that suited his fancy.

Aleister, Rose, and Lola

While Lilith was still an infant, her parents took her on a trip to China, where she died of typhoid fever. Rose descended more deeply into alcoholism after this, while Crowley suffered a series of health problems that necessitated surgery. In 1907, Rose gave birth to their second daughter, Lola, but even this was not enough to save the deeply troubled marriage, and two years later Crowley divorced Rose.

In 1912, Crowley was introduced to the Ordo Templi Orientis, a German occult society that practiced something near and dear to Crowley's heart: sex magic. Crowley introduced many of his own rituals, including a Gnostic Mass, into the Order's practices, and before long became head of the Order's British branch. He spent much of the remaining decade traveling around the United States, supporting his recreational drug use, sexual liaisons, "magickal" experimentation, and all other manner of licentious activities through his writings, paintings, and donations from his followers.

By the end of the decade, much of Crowley's fortune had been squandered on drugs, travels, and fruitless publishing ventures. But that did little to slow down his debauchery. In 1920, Crowley and his current mistress, Leah Hirsig, along with an entourage of men, women and children, moved into a dilapidated building in Cefalu, Sicily, which Crowley dubbed the Abbey of Thelema. He spent the next three years there indulging his passions for writing, painting, magick, sex, and drugs, often in full view of the children.

Crowley also used the Abbey to "instruct" his disciples, which included being subjugated to all manner of perverse rituals and bizarre teachings. The culmination of this depravity resulted in a disciple's act of bestiality with a goat. Another follower, Raoul Loveday, died of a liver infection after being forced to drink cat blood and urine at Crowley's behest. Loveday's widow made such a fuss to the press about her husband's death that the Italian government of Benito Mussolini expelled Crowley and his crew from the country in 1923.

From that point on, Crowley continued to travel around Europe, northern Africa, and the United States, promulgating his "magick" through writings and collaborations with other self-styled occultists, such as Sybil Leek, the author of the 1969 best-seller *Diary of a Witch;* magician Israel Regardie, who gained notoriety by exposing in print many of the Golden Dawn's secrets; and Gerald Gardner, founder of the modern-day Wiccan religion.

Crowley spent his last days at a Victorian boarding house in Hastings, England. Devastated financially from a failed libel lawsuit that forced him into bankruptcy, and ravaged physically from advanced respiratory disease and a lifetime of heavy drug usage, Crowley passed the time by socializing with friends and colleagues who continued to visit him right up until his time of death.

On December 1, 1947, he passed away quietly. Various reports say that Crowley uttered as his last words: "I am perplexed." Others report that he said, "I hate myself." But according to Patricia "Deirdre" MacAlpine, who had a son with Crowley some years earlier, and who visited him at the end, he said neither. Instead, she claimed, his moment of death was accompanied by a sudden gust of wind and a loud peal of thunder. Interestingly, Crowley's doctor died 24 hours later. It was widely reported in newspapers at the time that because the doctor had refused to continue his opiate prescription, Crowley had put a curse on him.

* * *

While Crowley has long since passed to a different world, his books and teachings still attract much attention today, as do the stories and legends about him that refuse to die. One of the most sensational tales kept in circulation is commonly called "The Paris Incident." It goes something like this:

One night in Paris in January 1914, Crowley and a devoted young acolyte sealed off the top floor of a small hotel for the purpose of invoking the god Pan. Crowley gave strict orders to friends who were waiting in a room below not to disturb the two of them during the ceremony under any circumstances. The ritual began and soon loud bangs and screaming were heard coming from the top floor. When finally the people waiting below decided enough was enough and broke down the door to the locked room, what they discovered was a nightmare. The room was a shambles, as if a wild beast had run amok. Crowley was huddled in a corner, naked and muttering gibberish, his ceremonial robe tattered and strewn aside. The acolyte lay dead in the center of the floor, the victim of an apparent heart attack. Both men were covered in bruises and scratches. A police inquiry ensued, but because Crowley could still not speak coherently about the incident, no charges were brought. Instead, Crowley was interred at a sanitarium, where he remained for four months.

The Paris Incident is one of the most controversial stories from Aleister Crowley's life and has been met throughout the years with a great deal of skepticism. There is no doubting, however, Crowley's devotion to the entity Pan. At his insistence, Crowley's cremation service in the town of Brighton included the reading of his original work, "Hymn to Pan." The local newspapers at the time referred to the service as a "Black Mass," and town officials declared that no such funeral would ever be held in their town again.

"I rave and I rape and I rip and I rend,
everlasting world without end." (Hymn to Pan)

Boleskine House

Although Aleister Crowley sold Boleskine House in 1913, its reputation as a house beset by evil spirits continued through decades of new ownerships. In 1962, Scottish businessman Dennis Loraine bought the house for his wife, Molly. As part of his new business venture, Loch Ness Foods, Loraine enlisted the financial aid of British film star George Sanders to build a pig farm on the property. However, nothing worked out as planned. Both Dennis and Molly descended into alcoholism, the pig rearing operation fizzled, the pigs died of starvation, and Dennis was convicted and imprisoned in one of the largest financial scandals in British history.

The next owner, retired Army Major Edward Grant, committed suicide in Crowley's old bedroom. In 1971, Led Zeppelin lead guitarist Jimmy Page—a Crowley memorabilia collector and aficionado—bought the house, but only lived in it a short time. He admitted in an interview with Rolling Stone that he felt "bad vibes" from the building.

During the making of the 2000 BBC documentary film "The Other Loch Ness Monster," filmmaker Garry Grant and his crew experienced a number of unsettling occurrences while at Boleskine, including nightmares about Crowley, phones ringing intermittently, an alarm clock going off unplanned at the same time every day, and unexplained ghostly fog appearing and ruining a series of still photos when there was no fog on the day they were taken. Most disturbing, though, was an onslaught of shrieking beetles that swarmed the crew during the filming of a segment about how Crowley's dogs were killed by beetles conjured through a magical spell by one of Crowley's adversaries. The beetles could not be identified by the Natural History Museum.

In December 2015, a large part of Boleskine House was destroyed by a fire. Luckily, it was unoccupied at the time.

2

The Conjuring Book

Jodie Parker had no idea what to get her daughter Sarah for Christmas. Given that this was the mid-1970s and personal electronics were limited to transistor radios, Jodie's choices of gifts were mostly clothes, games, and books. Sarah, who was 15, had plenty of clothes. Between Sarah and her two younger siblings, Peter and Amy, the family was well-stocked on games. That left books.

So the next day when Sarah was in school, Jodie perused the titles in her daughter's bedroom so as not to duplicate anything Sarah might have already read. Even though she knew about Sarah's interest in the occult, Jodie was still a little surprised at the vast array of occult books, candles, vestments, and other accouterments Sarah had accumulated. Jodie herself didn't think much of the occult one way or another, and figured this was just a teenage phase Sarah was going through. As she looked over the book titles, she noticed that none of them addressed the subject of conjuring. A light went off in her head. That was the answer! She'd get Sarah a book on conjuring, a gift she would actually be excited about, Jodie hoped.

On Christmas morning, Sarah was indeed delighted to receive her new book. It was a small paperback with instructions on how to conjure up nearly a hundred different demons. *Very cool*, thought Sarah. Over the next week, Sarah performed a few of the rituals, ones she had the right equipment for and could easily understand. To her disappointment, nothing out of the ordinary happened. She placed the book on her shelf and thought to herself, *maybe later*. What Sarah didn't know was that there was no need to try another spell later. She had succeeded in conjuring up *something* all right. It was just taking its time in making its presence known.

That time would be five months later, on a warm spring day in May. Sarah's parents, Jodie and Bill, had gone to a friend's house for dinner and cards. Before they left, they told their kids to get to bed at a decent time, as they had school the next day. Dutifully, at ten o'clock Peter and Amy went to bed while Sarah took a shower. After she finished, Sarah did a final check downstairs to make sure the doors were locked, the lights were out, and the radio was turned off. When she came back upstairs, she heard water running in the bathroom, but thinking it was Peter or Amy using the sink, she continued on to her room. After several minutes of hearing the water run continuously, Sarah went into the bathroom to find it empty, yet both faucets were on. She turned them off and started to go back to her room when she noticed the lights were on downstairs. And so was the radio. She quickly peeked in Amy's room, only to find her sister asleep. Then she checked on Peter, who was still awake. "Did you turn the lights and radio on downstairs?" she asked. Peter answered no. Cautiously, Sarah made her way back downstairs and turned off the lights and radio yet again.

When she returned upstairs, she was greeted once again by the sound of water running in the bathroom. Certain that Peter was pranking her, she angrily turned off the faucets and was just about to confront her brother when all of a sudden the radio started to blare downstairs and the lights all came back on. Sarah ran to Peter's room. "Do you hear that?" she asked. "Yeah," he answered. "I thought you wanted it on." She pressed him further about the faucets, but just as he was denying even being out of bed, the radio started changing stations. Sarah's first thought was that her parents had come home. She went down fully expecting to see them, but instead she saw to her shock the radio dial moving back and forth by itself. On the verge of panic now, Sarah quickly turned off the radio and lights and fled upstairs. As she neared the top, she felt an icy-cold hand touch her shoulder. She suppressed a scream and ran to her bedroom, shut the door, and dived into her bed. At that very moment, Sarah heard the unmistakable sound of footsteps leaving her room and walking out to the hall, even though her door remained closed.

Sarah lay still in bed, her covers pulled up tight, and listened as chaos seemed to break out downstairs. First a door slammed, followed by the sound of furniture being slid around, and then, crazily, unexplainably, came the sound of furniture being *thrown* around. Sarah was positive someone was in the house but she was too scared to move. She closed her eyes and the next thing she knew someone, or something, pulled her hair. She opened her eyes to an empty room. Then the invisible hand yanked her hair two more times, hard enough to make her eyes water. This time Sarah did scream. Then she jumped up and ran to Peter's room.

The noises continued at a frantic rate. Crashing, slamming, sliding. Footsteps that sounded like they went around in circles. Unintelligible whispering. Sarah and Peter listened to it all, terrified, while trying to figure out what to do next. Sarah wanted to call the police, but Peter argued that they would just get in trouble if the police came and found no one in the house. So they called their parents at their friend's house. But just as Sarah and Peter feared, when Jodie and Bill came home, not only were no strangers found in the house, but the downstairs was in perfect order, not a single piece of furniture out of place. Though Amy told her parents the next morning that she had heard all the commotion, too, Jodie and Bill tried to convince the children that they had been simply hearing things.

Two nights later, Sarah and Peter were again alone in the house while their parents and Amy were out. This time Peter had just taken a shower when he heard the radio on downstairs. Thinking Sarah was down there, he walked down the steps to join her but found only his dog in the living room. The dog was visibly upset. Normally very laid back, now it was snarling viciously at *something*, but nothing Peter could see. The memory of the other night still fresh in his mind, Peter raced back upstairs to his bed. About five minutes later he heard the unmistakable sound of furniture once again being thrown around downstairs.

Sarah heard it too. She later recounted how as her fear grew stronger, the noises seemed to grow louder. As she lay in her bed, too terrified to move, her hands balled up into tight fists, she saw out of the corner of her eye a hazy purplish mass. But when she tried to look directly at it, it disappeared, only to reappear again in her periphery. Suddenly, she felt a man's hand around her left fist. It tried to pry it open, but as Sarah fought to keep her fist closed the invisible hand grabbed her arm and tried to pull her out of bed. Screaming, she broke loose from her unseen attacker and ran into Peter's room.

The siblings quickly agreed that they needed to get out of the house. Both felt an impending sense of evil all around them. They didn't want to go downstairs to get to the front door, but they had no other choice as the windows in their rooms were up too high. So they decided to run as quickly as they could straight out the door. Thankfully, nothing blocked their way as they raced out of the house. Neither took the time to look around, but Peter remembers hearing loud buzzing, static most likely, coming from the radio. Without a specific plan in mind, the duo ran down the road leading to the local college campus. Their relief at being out of the house was short-lived when a group of dogs came out of nowhere and started running toward them. Peter and Sarah watched in disbelief as the dogs gained on them —and then ran backwards! At the same time, birds screeched wildly from the trees on the left side of the road. Birds at 11:00 at night!

Afraid to slow down in the midst of their surreal surroundings, and unable to shake the feeling that something from the house was following them, Peter and Sarah raced on until they saw a street lamp. For some reason, they knew they had to get to the light of the street lamp. But as they got closer, a force enveloped them, slowed their progress, and tried to push them down. "There was no air to breathe," Sarah later recounted. Through sheer tenacity, they reached the street lamp and immediately felt the pressure around them lift. The birds stopped screeching, and an overall sense of safety descended on them. But after a few minutes, the light began to dim and the birds began to screech again. Peter and Sarah knew they had to keep going. They took off running until they finally starting seeing cars and buildings. They stopped at a convenience store, where they called their parents and explained what had happened and where they were.

Everything back home, of course, appeared to be normal when Sarah and Peter returned with their parents. But this time, Jodie and Bill, even though they had yet to experience anything strange themselves, believed that something unexplainable had happened to their children and reached out for help. They had heard of paranormal investigators Ed and Lorraine Warren from a speaking appearance the Warrens made on campus a few months earlier. Since the Warrens lived in Connecticut also, Jodie hoped she could convince them to come out to the house.

After a frustrating game of phone tag, during which the lines between the Parkers and the Warrens kept mysteriously going "dead," arrangements were finally made for the Warrens to come out and investigate.

The Warrens got right to work. Ed interviewed the family members about the strange goings-on while Lorraine walked through the house hoping to discern any supernatural or psychic presence with her clairvoyant ability. While she immediately picked up negative energy vibes downstairs, it was the upstairs area, particularly Sarah's bedroom, that exuded the strongest energy. In fact, Lorraine didn't even try to enter Sarah's bedroom, as something unseen "pushed" on Lorraine's head and shoulders the closer she got to it. Downstairs, Ed had heard enough. Between what the Parkers had just told him and Lorraine's discernment, he had little doubt a demonic presence was in the house. He asked the Parkers to leave for an hour, during which time, he advised, he would try to "take care of the matter."

Ed and Lorraine then went about performing a binding ritual in each room of the house. This process involved sprinkling holy water in the corners of each room and commanding any infesting spirit to show itself or move on. The ritual went without incident in the basement and all rooms on the first floor. But as soon as the Warrens started going upstairs, a heavy feeling of dread enveloped them. A strong rotting smell assaulted their noses, and as they looked up, a shadow flitted across the top of the stairs, followed by the jarring noise of a door slamming. Shaken but determined, the Warrens pressed on. About halfway up the stairs, they were stopped in their tracks by an invisible force that pushed against them. Afraid of tumbling backwards, they retreated to the base of the stairs. Ed splashed a liberal amount of holy water on the steps, and the pressure immediately abated, allowing the Warrens to go up to the second floor.

Again they started the binding ritual, beginning in Amy's room. Encountering no difficulties, they moved on to Peter's room where, again, nothing unusual presented itself. When they opened the door to Sarah's room, however, it was a much different story. Immediately they were overcome with a feeling of misery, as if something in the room not only wanted to demoralize the Warrens, but gain their sympathy. Ed was having nothing of it, though, having experienced this ploy before. With renewed determination, he pressed forward into the freezing cold bedroom and splashed holy water in all four corners. Then, holding a crucifix in front of him, he commanded in a strong voice, "In the name of God, show yourself now — or leave!" He repeated the command, this time threatening an exorcism if the spirit didn't leave. The response was instantaneous. The temperature in the room steadily rose until it reached its normal state. And the feeling of misery and doom drained away, indicating to the Warrens that the spell had been broken. The only task that remained was getting rid of the objects in the room that had attracted the evil in the first place. Ed and Lorraine quickly collected all of Sarah's books, candles, vestments, and other occult paraphernalia and took them out to the trash cans. Then, as one last precaution before leaving, they "sealed" Sarah's room by reciting a prayer of sanctification.

Just as they were finishing up, the Parkers returned home. While assuring them that the negative spirit had been expelled, the Warrens were also adamant that it could easily return—stronger than before even. To prevent this from happening, Ed explained, the Parkers needed to project positive energy into the house to counteract negative spirit energy. He strongly advised doing positive things together as a family, like going to church once a week, and avoiding things that could bring disharmony or negative emotions to the family.

And, of course, no more demon-conjuring books for Christmas.

* * *

"Spirits don't necessarily come when you want them to. Once you invite them in, they come when THEY want to. It could be 3:00 o'clock in the morning when you're all alone. Imagine lying in bed all alone and suddenly feeling something crawl into bed with you."

– Ed Warren, demonologist

3

The Curse

Carla Rozini and her husband Marco were well-to-do small business owners in Bologna, Italy. Married for eight years, they were still deeply in love with each other, vibrant in their faith, and successful at work. But it was painfully apparent to them that there was still one part of their lives that simply was not to be—bringing forth their own children. So after much prayer and consideration, they finally decided to adopt a baby boy and girl.

Luckily for Carla and Marco, the adoption process went through without a hitch, and the Rozinis were soon the elated parents of Antonio and Lucia. But not everyone was happy about the Rozinis' newest additions. The Rozinis had always been very generous in helping out members of their family who needed financial assistance. But now with two children suddenly in the picture, murmurs began circulating that the money would dry up, as well as any future inheritances. Among those worried were Carla's brother and his wife. Both were long-time students of the occult, but the wife was also a practicing witch who decided to take matters into her own hands by putting a curse on Carla. She freely admitted this years later after divorcing Carla's brother.

Unaware that she had been targeted, Carla began feeling ill about a month after the curse had been placed. Having been healthy all her life, it came as a surprise to learn she was suffering from heart, spleen, and liver problems. But more disconcerting was the absence of any solutions. Doctors would prescribe a remedy only to have it completely fail.

Along with her physical ailments, Carla also began experiencing spiritual difficulties. For as long as she could remember, Carla had been a fervent churchgoer and ardent in her prayer life. Now she found it impossible to pray and she couldn't stand the thought of setting foot in a church. More troubling were her increasing thoughts and temptations to outright curse and blaspheme God, saints, angels, and anything that hinted of holiness. This caused immense heartache to her husband Marco as well.

Carla's problems persisted for ten years until in 1988 she had her gallbladder removed at the suggestion of a surgeon. Her health problems still did not improve, so her doctor next suggested she visit a famous thermal spa located in a neighboring region. Carla did, but instead of healing, her body became wracked with even more excruciating pain. She went to see a local physician who, after examining her, studying her past medical records, and finding nothing physically wrong, asked if she was "a believer." Carla answered yes, at which the physician recommended she see a priest, as he told her, "Your sufferings go beyond anything that medical science can cure."

Carla and Marco returned home, physically and spiritually exhausted. They had met several times with a priest while still at the spa, but his counseling and deliverance prayers did little to alleviate Carla's physical symptoms or spiritual battles. His final advice was that they should contact their bishop and ask for the name of an exorcist. Desperate to try anything, they asked the bishop for help, and on August 16, 1988, Carla had her first appointment with diocesan exorcist Father Spano. During this and two subsequent sessions with Carla, the priest aimed his deliverance prayers at breaking the bonds between Carla and those individuals in her life who meant her harm. This included not only the sister-in-law who practiced witchcraft, but also a friend who was jealous over the Rozinis' successful adoptions, as well as several domestic workers who were fearful of losing their jobs in the wake of the Rozinis' expanding family.

Next, Father Spano directed his efforts at "cleaning" the Rozinis' country home. Carla and Marco had always wondered about the eerie and unexplainable noises that pervaded the house, but it wasn't until they were looking deep into family records for answers to Carla's plight that they discovered the previous owners of the house were members of a satanic cult and had hosted black masses and other satanic rituals in the house. Father Spano suggested they search the house for any occult objects that may have been deliberately hidden by the former residents. To the Rozinis' shock, the search produced a small box of charms and amulets that had been stuffed in the back of a guest closet. Father Spano burned the items, and then performed an exorcism of the premises that immediately brought a sense of peace and quiet to the abode.

Unfortunately, neither the deliverance prayers nor the exorcism of the house helped Carla. She was still plagued by inexplicable illnesses and the sense of revulsion toward anything religious. After careful consideration of everything he had learned about the case thus far, and after consulting with a psychologist who regularly helped him discern true mental illness in many of the people who came to him, Father Spano made the decision to perform an exorcism on Carla herself.

Unlike in the movies where an exorcism is often "one and done," in real life Catholic exorcisms are done over a period of time, sometimes even taking as long as years before the victim is completely relieved. In Carla's case, it took several exorcism sessions before the demon possessing her became fully enraged enough to show himself, at which point Father Spano could address it directly. Invoking the names of Jesus Christ, Mary, St. Michael the Archangel and other saints, the priest then commanded:

"I break every occult tie of black magic—sorcery, curse, and hex—between you, foul spirit, and Carla. I bind every power of this spirit and I command him to leave Carla . . ."

Carla finally felt relief after this exorcism. She found it easier to pray and was actually able to attend church with the help of her husband. The demon had not left yet, but it was apparent it was getting more desperate. At the next exorcism, it became so enraged at Father Spano's reading of the Psalms and recitation of the Rosary that it offered a "deal." It would quit blaspheming and "only" insult Father Spano. Needless to say, the exorcisms continued.

Finally, at a subsequent session, after having been beaten down yet again by the ritual and prayers, the demon offered a better deal. "Leave me the following six relatives [and named those he wanted], and I will leave Carla." At this, the priest invoked the Holy Spirit to break every bond with black magic, curses, and witchcraft with every one of the six individuals whom the demon wanted for his own. Finally, Father Spano entrusted each person by name to Mary the Mother of God. The demon became furious and screamed out: "If you take them away from me, what will be left for me? What will I become?"

It still took many more exorcisms before Carla was completely freed from her tormentors. As the rituals went on, it became apparent that multiple demons possessed Carla, and were under the command of one particularly powerful demon. Father Spano was well acquainted with this demon but declined to release its name publicly so as not to bestow on it any further fame.

Carla continued to heal spiritually and physically throughout her years of undergoing the exorcisms. Her family thrived, and she and Marco successfully raised their children into adulthood without any other catastrophes. And what became of the family members and acquaintances who wished them harm years before? No doubt the ill-willers learned their lesson upon hearing of the demon's request for them by name. Carla and Marco experienced no further trouble from them, and much of the enmity between them and the Rozinis dispersed over time.

* * *

"Curses invoke evil, and the origin of all evil is demonic. When curses are spoken with true perfidy, especially if there is a blood relationship between the one who casts them and the accursed, the outcome can be terrible."

– **Fr. Gabriele Amorth, former chief exorcist of Rome**

The Business of Curses

Fascination with the occult has become a national phenomenon in Italy. It is estimated that there are 20,000 to 30,000 "magi" or magicians offering their professional services, which covers everything from spell casting to divination to demon expulsion. It is a lucrative business to be in, with reports of Italians spending more than $20 million a year on preternatural guidance and magical solutions. "Italy is very fertile soil for these practices because of the way its pre-Christian pagan culture has mixed with Catholicism," explains Luigi Satriani, an ethnologist at the University of Rome.

Removing curses is one of the more popular services offered by magi. Milka Fratnik, an occult practitioner in

Rome, is a specialist in curse removal. She is kept busy with a steady stream of clients, many of them businessmen and politicians who have found themselves on the receiving end of an enemy's jealousy or wrath. The signs of being cursed are sometimes subtle, such as a vague illness or a run of unexplainable bad luck. Sometimes they are more obvious, like a dead bird with a nail through its heart left on a doorstep. What Fratnik says she can do for her clients is turn the "negative energy" back on the enemy. "In the end, the enemy will destroy himself," she says.

Fratnik and a few others like her claim to be religious and God-fearing as well as skilled in the mystical arts. In Fratnik's tastefully-decorated office there are religious paintings on the wall and a Bible on a coffee table in addition to volumes on magic filling her bookshelves and a deck of Tarot cards on her desk. Fratnik sees no conflict with this dual viewpoint, and insists she is simply a facilitator for helping people make good decisions and getting them out of bad situations.

Another such maga is Annamaria Ammendola. Her specialty is casting out demons and evil spirits. She too claims to be a religious person, and she keeps in close contact with the local priest in her town, with whom she exchanges stories and trades advice. One of her more sensational cases involved a woman, Pasqualina Meale, who for several months had been plagued by a sickness that neither her hometown doctor nor specialists in Naples and Rome could identify. Not being able to sleep or eat, she grew increasingly emaciated and haggard. Months passed until, finally, frightened family members took her to see Ammendola.

Ammendola took one look at Pasqualina and knew without a doubt that someone had put a curse on the young woman. She prodded Pasqualina's memory: Did anything happen right before you got sick that might have initiated someone putting a curse on you? There was one incident, Pasqualina recalled. One day while at work—she was a secretary for the municipal council in her town—a stranger came up to her desk and tried to get her to tamper with the voter registration lists. She refused, of course, and the man angrily stormed out of the office. It was shortly after that when she came down with this mysterious ailment.

Ammendola had seen cases like this before and knew that "fixing" it was not as simple as a routine curse reversal. A demon had taken possession of Pasqualina, she feared, and if it wasn't expelled it would continue to make the poor woman sicker until death overtook her. Ammendola prepared herself by entering into three days of intense prayer and concentration, gathering her "cosmic energy," as she put it. Then she went to work casting out the demon. On the seventh day, Pasqualina vomited up a golf ball-sized wad of human hair. The demon left and the curse was broken.

Half the wad, framed and matted, now hangs on the wall of Ammendola's office. The other half she gave to her priest friend. The two have come to an understanding, which Ammendola sums up simply: "The priests have their business, and I have mine."

4

The Wish

Another Friday night alone on the couch. Alicia was used to them. She had long made do with beach books and popcorn movies to pass the time week after week. Still, she longed for the romantic relationships that so many of her friends had. Even if they hadn't worked out, at least there was the drama and excitement of falling in and out of love. Alicia was starting to doubt that she'd ever experience those feelings. She knew that part of her problem, in addition to being shy, was that she was picky. She didn't want just any old guy. She wanted Mr. Perfect.

Her eyes lit on the curio shelf next to her television, in particular to a gray clay oil-burning lamp that had been perched there for the last six months. Her uncle had brought it back from a trip to the Middle East, where he was told it was a very old and valuable artifact. Looking at the small, rough-sided object with black burn marks, Alicia doubted it could be worth that much. It certainly wasn't that attractive. But it was a conversation piece. She only wished she had someone in her life with whom to converse.

Wish. Wish. Rub the lamp and make a wish!

The voice in her head startled her. Where had that come from? Boredom, she supposed. She turned her attention back to the television with a sigh. All those channels and yet nothing that held her interest. As she channel surfed, she caught herself stealing glances at the little lamp. Despite the noise from the TV, she could still hear that voice in the back of her mind—a masculine but congenial voice. *Rub the lamp and make a wish. Go ahead. It's fun!*

Really? She asked herself, chuckling. *Do I really think I have a magic lamp here? Obviously I've watched Aladdin too many times.*

Alicia tried concentrating on an inane sitcom rerun but found herself more and more obsessing over the lamp. *Maybe I should try making a wish,* she thought. *It's just harmless fun. Besides, I'll just keep thinking about it until I do.*

Switching off the TV, Alicia snatched the lamp off the bookcase and started rubbing it between her hands. Now she just had to decide what to wish for. In the stories, a genie usually popped out and granted three wishes. A genie! She giggled at the thought of a swarthy, bare-chested man suddenly materializing in front of her. Maybe she should just wish for that! Alicia went through a mental checklist of possibilities: a handsome husband, lots of money, a perfect job . . . Then a sudden bolt of inspiration hit her: She would wish for *all* her wishes to come true! She rubbed the lamp and made her wish.

Nothing happened, of course. No smoke swirled out of the lamp. No fireworks or earthquakes shook the house. And no hunky genie appeared. Alicia expected as much with her rational mind, but her imaginative mind was still a little disappointed. It apparently was still working, too, as she continued to hear that voice in her head. *Good, good, good!*

With a shrug, Alicia put the lamp back on the shelf and went to bed. *Maybe a genie will come to me in my dreams*, she thought as she drifted off. Later that night, Alicia did have a dream, but it wasn't what she had hoped for. She found herself standing in a long line of people outside a large, nondescript building. A sign by the front entrance advertised "Free Lunch!" The line inched along until Alicia was finally inside what appeared to be a cafeteria. She grabbed a tray like everyone else and began to help herself to plates of food when suddenly a man's voice boomed out: "Stop! What are you doing?" Alicia looked up. Towering over her was a tall, olive-skinned man with a neatly-trimmed beard and mustache. Though he appeared angry at her, she couldn't help feel an immediate attraction to him. She blushed as she answered, "I'm getting lunch."

"You haven't paid," the man said, his dark eyes flashing and boring into her.

"But the sign says it's free," said Alicia.

"There is no such thing as a free lunch, A-lee-shee-a. You only get what you pay for. Why don't you make me an offer?"

Alicia tried to speak but no words would come out of her mouth.

"No matter. I already know what you want." Then he laughed the vilest laugh Alicia had ever heard, chilling her to the bone.

This isn't real. I must be dreaming, she thought. *I want to wake up. I want to wake up!*

Suddenly the dream ended and Alicia awoke with a start. Disoriented and frightened, she took a few minutes sitting up in bed with the light on before convincing herself it was okay to go back to sleep. Thankfully, she had no more dreams that night.

The next morning at work, Alicia found herself more annoyed than usual at a loquacious colleague in the cubicle next to her. Debbie was in fine form this morning, babbling on and on with another co-worker about something totally inane, punctuating the conversation every so often with a piercing, high-pitched laugh that sent waves of pain into Alicia's already headache-plagued skull, compliments of the previous night's interrupted sleep. As she put her head down on her desk and covered her ears, she thought to herself, *I wish Debbie would stuff it!*

No sooner had the thought left her head than she heard coughing coming from Debbie's cubicle. The coughing grew louder and morphed into sounds of gagging. Alicia looked over her wall and saw Debbie doubled over, in obvious distress like she was choking on something. "Debbie, what's wrong?" Alicia asked, concerned. Debbie stood and waved her off, then quickly made a run for the bathroom. When she returned, she looked like a miserable wrung-out wreck. "I have to go home," she croaked to Alicia, and grabbing her purse and coat, she abruptly left the office. *Strange,* thought Alicia. Even though Debbie drove her crazy most of the time, she still hoped her co-worker would be all right.

Exhausted by a long day at the office and the headache that never completely went away, Alicia called it a night early. She had been enjoying a peaceful sleep when around 2:30 a.m. she was slightly awakened by the sensation of a person sliding into bed next to her. It had the muscular and hairy feel of a man, and because she thought she was still asleep and dreaming, Alicia didn't become instantly alarmed. The man started to caress her in an intimate manner, and Alicia found herself enjoying the experience. After several moments she turned to look at her mystery lover and was horrified to see the imposing man from last night's lunch line dream.

Alicia screamed as he loomed over her with an evil smirk and glittering dark eyes. "No!" she yelled. "Go away!" When he didn't move, Alicia felt her defenses weaken and tears stream down her face. "I just wish you would go back where you came from," she managed between sobs. At that, the man instantly vanished, and Alicia was left trembling with fear and doubting her sanity. Though it was still the middle of the night, she jumped out of bed and hurried to the kitchen, turning on every light along the way. There she stayed until dawn.

Unfortunately for Alicia, her troubles were just beginning. While the swarthy man-phantom didn't appear again, other disturbing phenomena invaded Alicia's days and nights. The air in the house became thick and unpleasant. A sense of gloom pervaded the atmosphere and weighed down on Alicia's own disposition. Room temperatures changed dramatically on their own—from freezing cold one minute to hellaciously hot the next.

At night Alicia would be awakened by skittering sounds on the roof, as if small animals were running rampant above her head. Sometimes the sounds were closer and more direct, like scratching noises from within the wall by her bed, or loud pounding on the walls that shook pictures and shelves. Small objects would go missing, like the time a pair of earrings disappeared from Alicia's dresser top only to be found hours later on top of the garbage can.

But the most horrifying occurrences were the manifestations. They occurred often and without warning. A black shadow figure would appear out of nowhere, flitting around the house from room to room. Then it would disappear in the blink of an eye. Once Alicia was awakened by the black figure standing at the side of her bed. She screamed and the phantom vanished in a hazy swirl of smoke. If waking nightmares weren't enough, her sleep-induced dreams were terrifying as well. She was plagued by dreams of being chased by unseen monsters, and once she had a dream in which unknown assailants were pressuring her to sign a contract that she didn't want to sign.

At the same time all of this was happening, Alicia's attention was drawn increasingly to the little gray lamp, along with the menacing invitation that seemed to be always in her mind: *Rub the lamp. Make a wish.* Alicia usually deflected those thoughts easily enough—especially with everything that happened since the first time she gave in. But one day the lamp caught her attention in a new way. It was vibrating on the shelf, so violently that Alicia feared it would fall off. She rushed over and picked it up, and then nearly dropped it herself when she felt an electric-like pulse surge from it into her hands. She quickly placed it back on the shelf and watched as it continued to shake, rapidly at first and then less and less as it finally quieted to a standstill.

Not surprisingly, Alicia started spending more and more time away from her house. But even when she was away, bad luck and misfortune seemed to be her constant companions. Her computer would crash at work while everyone else's worked fine. A package she had been eagerly waiting for never arrived. She was always tripping and bumping into things. On two occasions she nearly fell down a flight of stairs. One of those times she could have sworn someone pushed her, though no one was in sight. She took a good look at herself in the mirror one day after showering and couldn't believe the number of bruises all over her body.

But it wasn't until she was nearly killed in a car accident by a maniac driver who appeared out of nowhere and missed crashing into her by inches that she gave up all hope of things eventually getting better. She knew they wouldn't, not on their own. Alicia needed help in fighting whatever evil she had unknowingly unleashed. She didn't know what it was she up against, but she knew where it had come from: the lamp.

Alicia thought her story would sound crazy to paranormal investigator John Zaffis, so when he agreed to come out to her house, she allowed herself a glimmer of hope that maybe her nightmare would soon be over. He had told her to put the lamp outside until he could get there in a few days, telling her that might settle things down a bit inside the house. To Alicia's pleasant surprise, there were fewer disturbances since she relocated the lamp. The atmosphere seemed a little less heavy and morbid, but she was still troubled by bad dreams. When John finally arrived at the house and examined the lamp, any fears she had of appearing crazy went by the wayside. If anything, John's explanation of what was going on made *him* seem like the nut job.

"You have a genie on your hands," he stated matter-of-factly.

Alicia was dumbstruck. Sure, she had jokingly fantasized about a genie coming out of her little "magic lamp," but never in a million years expected it to really happen. And if it was a genie haunting her, it certainly wasn't like the friendly, slap-happy genie in *Aladdin.* Whatever it was that came out of her lamp was cruel and hateful.

John explained that what they were actually dealing with was a *djinn* (also spelled jinn), an inhuman spirit whose kind has co-existed with humans since antiquity. As talked about in early Arabic mythology and later in Islamic theology, the djinn are said to be supernatural creatures who reside in their own realm but have the ability to cross over into ours and interfere in human affairs. This primarily happens when they are conjured via magical rites or invoked specifically to perform certain tasks. The djinn are said to be superb shapeshifters, often appearing as snakes or black dogs, but other times as demons, fairies, ghosts, shadow people, insects, or even beautiful, seductive people, such as the handsome man who invaded Alicia's bed.

Like other created species, the djinn have free will and, accordingly, some choose to be good and some choose to be evil. As is so often the case, it is bad news and bad people that garner the most notoriety, and it is no different with the djinn. Stories abound of malicious, vengeful, violent djinn destroying people's lives by bringing bad luck, illness, tragedy, and even death to those unfortunate enough to cross their paths. But what about "good djinn?" Could a person call on them for favors or services, like a healing for instance? Islamic scholars say no, as djinn and humans are two separate entities with two separate worlds in which to live. Any attempt to cross those worlds is, from a theological viewpoint, wrong, and from a practical viewpoint, dangerous.

One thing all scholars and paranormal experts agree on is that djinn can't be trusted. As paranormal expert Rosemary Ellen Guiley says in her treatise *A Short Course on the Djinn*, "Even when granting favors, they have a trickster nature and can twist events for the worse." In Alicia's case, it may have seemed at first that her wishes were coming true, but soon the events in her life became chaotic and horrifying. "It's all about deals with them," John explained to her. "They promise to deliver what you want, but they want something, usually human energy, in return." And they'll create a plethora of problems and pandemonium to raise it. In fact, many paranormal researchers like Rosemary Guiley believe the djinn are responsible for a great number of reported hauntings, poltergeist activity, and full-out possessions typically attributed to demons of the Judeo-Christian traditions.

Alicia was still confused. How exactly did this spirit, this *djinn*, get trapped inside her little lamp? And how did it get out? She didn't make any "deals" with it. At least as far as she knew.

John told her that most likely someone in the Middle East, where the lamp originally came from, "bound" the djinn to the lamp by means of an occult ritual. It remained dormant in the lamp until it spied an opportunity for release. That opportunity came when Alicia answered its siren song to make a wish. It didn't matter that Alicia didn't really believe she was asking a genie for a wish, or that she was participating in an act of occult magic. Her subtle consent was enough for the spirit to break its psychic chains and make her life a living hell.

Fortunately for Alicia, John was able to re-chain the djinn to the lamp by declaring Alicia's debt "paid" and performing a binding ritual, after which he encased the lamp in a clear acrylic box so no one else could touch it and compromise the binding. He then arranged for two exorcisms to be performed: one on Alicia and one on her house to rid her completely of any negative energy that may have remained behind. Alicia's life went back to normal after that, but she never forgot the harsh lesson learned: Be careful what you wish for. Someone, or *something*, may be listening.

* * *

"There are those who would like to get in contact with these beings and utilize their capacity . . . Now there is no guarantee that what they tell you will be right because these jinns are very mischievous with a little bit of right and plenty wrong."

– Dr. Waffie Mohammed, Islamic scholar

5

The Haunted Ouija Board

Growing up in a middle-class Midwestern suburb in the 1990s, Susan and Jake Miller led idyllic teenage lives. When they weren't hanging out with their friends, they engaged in friendly sibling rivalry by trying to outdo each other in the art of fear-mongering. They played Bloody Mary, told scary stories in the dark, pulled squeamish pranks on one another, and occasionally—armed with candles, paper, and pins with which to prick their fingers—challenged each other to a game of Midnight Man. But their favorite goosebump-inducing activity by far was using their Ouija board to talk to spirits of the dead.

The Ouija board was a gift given to them by their aunt. Though it was made of cheap cardboard and plastic, to the Miller kids it was a priceless treasure. They took turns bringing it to sleepovers and parties, but most often used it together in one of their darkened bedrooms, usually after their parents—who weren't crazy about the board—had gone to bed. They spent hours "talking" to dead celebrities, deceased relatives, and any other passing spirits that came their way. The plastic planchette slithered around the board effortlessly under their practiced fingers, and only at the end of their sessions did they argue about who had been moving the pointer more.

One day Susan and Jake decided to make their Ouija game more interesting—and hopefully more scary. Their bedroom summonings were fun, and sometimes a little creepy, but both of them believed deep down that they were only playing a game. And games can grow stale without new "levels" introduced. Those feelings led to their decision to use the Ouija in the scariest place they could think of: a local cemetery said to be haunted by the spirits of gangsters who had been murdered there decades ago.

Convincing their friend Katie to join them, mostly because she had a car, Susan and Jake slipped out of their house one warm summer night and drove over with Katie to the woods bordering the cemetery, the Ouija board snug in Susan's backpack. They parked inside a heavily forested area to avoid being caught by police who regularly cruised by the cemetery looking for late-night intruders. The kids had visited these woods many times during the day and knew well the way to the graveyard, even if it did look eerily different in the dead of night. They were reminded of all the stories they had heard—stories about drug deals, prostitution, and witchcraft occurring in these woods—and wondered, briefly, if they were more in danger here or in the cemetery.

Finally, they saw glimpses of headstones and hurried the rest of the way through the dark canopy of trees. Once inside the cemetery, the trio settled on a comfortable-looking patch of ground and prepared for their conjuring session. Jake unrolled a blanket for them to sit on, Susan removed the Ouija board from her backpack, and Katie propped a flashlight up against the nearest headstone to give them at least some illumination in the fog that swirled around them. They sat in a circle around the board, put their fingertips in place on the planchette, and recited the "summoning rhyme" they always used to open a session.

Ouija Ouija Ouija,
Can the spirits come and play?
Ouija Ouija Ouija,
We haven't got all day.

Normally Susan and Jake would have to recite the verses about a dozen times before getting an answer. But tonight they weren't even through the third round before the planchette started making circles around the board. Susan asked who was there, and the planchette suddenly stopped. Just then they heard footsteps approaching them from the path they had taken out of the woods. Katie took her hands off the board, grabbed the flashlight, and turned it off. They waited in silence for several minutes until Susan finally whispered, "Let's keep–" She gasped as the planchette lurched to the side. Katie clicked the flashlight back on and watched as Susan and Jake's fingers swirled around the board, the planchette stopping at the letters:
B L A C K
"Do you think it's a name?" asked Jake. "Maybe it's on one of the headstones."

The planchette started moving again. This time it added the letters:

H E N

"Black hen? What does that mean?" asked Susan.

"Maybe it's a nickname for one of the gangsters who died here," suggested Jake.

Suddenly the planchette started moving again, faster and faster, stopping on the same letters, over and over.

B L A C K H E N B L A C K H E N B L A C K H E

In none of their previous Ouija board sessions had Susan and Jake experienced anything like this. The planchette was moving with a swiftness and power that demanded their entire concentration to keep their fingers attached to it. This time they didn't have to argue about who was moving the planchette. They knew without a doubt there was another force at play with them.

Something else was happening too. A brown spot appeared in the center of the board. As Jake and Susan watched in amazement, the spot turned a deep black while the smooth surface of the board began to warp and crinkle. A crack appeared in the center of the black mass, releasing wispy slivers of pungent smoke into the air. Susan, Jake, and Katie jumped up from the blanket in unison and ducked behind a headstone, their eyes still focused on the smoldering board. As they whispered among themselves about what to do next, the planchette, abandoned by Jake and Susan when they fled, suddenly lurched forward and slowly moved on its own toward the center of the board. Transfixed, the teens watched in horror until the smoke morphed into flames and engulfed the entire board. Then they ran.

The trio raced back through the woods to Katie's parked car. They dove in and were driving out when Susan remembered she had left her backpack behind.

"No way are we going back," said Katie. "We can get it tomorrow morning."

"We didn't close the board," muttered Jake, referring to the practice of ending each Ouija session with the word Goodbye. "We messed up."

Susan and Jake convinced Katie to stay the rest of the night at their house. It was already 4:00 a.m., so a few more hours wouldn't make much of a difference. At 8:00 the next morning, the three of them drove back to the cemetery. There they found Susan's backpack right where she had left it, the contents undisturbed. Next to it lay the Ouija board, twisted and charred in a pile of ash. Jake wrapped up the board, intending to keep it as proof of its supernatural abilities. He and Susan agreed to tell their parents, believing it best to let someone else know about it. Someone with authority.

Their parents, Alec and Maggie, weren't thrilled. Either about the Ouija board experience or the fact that they snuck out of the house in the middle of the night and spent three hours in a cemetery in a crime-ridden part of town. Jake and Susan were grounded, and the Ouija board thrown into the trash. Too tired to argue, the siblings went to their separate bedrooms and collapsed into their beds.

Several hours later they were rudely awakened by the screech of a smoke detector. As they groggily stumbled out of their rooms, they saw their father looking up at the hall ceiling, a puzzled look on his face. "There's no fire," he assured them. "Probably just needs new batteries." As if to confirm their father's theory, the alarm suddenly stopped. But then, seconds later, the one in the living room went off. Then the one in the kitchen. Their father spent the better part of that Saturday changing all the batteries in all the alarms. But it was all for naught. A couple of hours later, the alarms began screeching again. They started in one end of the house and came on one after the other, as if switched on deliberately by some unseen passerby. By the end of the day, a half-dozen smoke alarms lay dismantled, batteries removed, on the kitchen table.

The next morning it wasn't a smoke alarm that woke Susan and John, but their mother yelling. "Bad dog, Quincy! Bad dog!" They found her in the living room cleaning ash off the cream-colored carpet. Ash that belonged to the discarded Ouija board, now lying in the middle of the floor. On a nearby footstool was the melted planchette. Seeing them standing in the doorway, their mother just shook her head and muttered, "Quincy must have dragged this out of the trash when we were sleeping. What a mess!" When she was done, she put the Ouija in a new trash bag and took it out to the garage. "At least he can't drag it back in now," she said. Jake and Susan looked at each other, the same thought in their heads: Quincy didn't take that board out of the trash.

From that point on, strange incidents began to happen to all family members. Maggie found herself locked in the bathroom one morning when she was alone in the house, even though the door had no lock on it. Alec was besieged by the constant smell of rotting meat, though no other person in the house could smell it, nor was any source for the smell ever found. Jake was suddenly plagued by nosebleeds, a previously rare occurrence for him. And Susan developed a crippling fear of her closet. The idea would not leave her head that something evil had taken up residence in there. Even Quincy started acting oddly. He hardly touched his food, and he refused to come into the house unless forced.

But it was an event one evening at dinnertime, when everyone was together, that made them admit something very bad had invaded their home. They had just finished eating when Quincy jumped up from under the table and started barking at something in the hallway leading to the back door. Alec went over and startled the others when he said in a loud voice: "What are you doing in there?" At the far end of the hall stood a tall shadowy figure. Alec told Maggie to call 911, at which point the shadow man slowly moved further down the darkened hall. The family listened for the door to close, but it never came. When police arrived a short time later, they found no evidence of a forced entry, nor any signs of an intruder still on the premises.

After that night, the paranormal activity in the Miller house increased in intensity. The shadow man appeared two more times, once in the kitchen and once in the backyard. Susan's bed began to shake violently in the middle of the night. Putrid odors fouled the air constantly, and electrical devices turned on and off by themselves. When the family awoke one morning to find the discarded, charred Ouija board back in their living room, lying atop a dark ashen stain on the carpet, the warped planchette next to it, they knew they needed outside help.

Though not a particularly religious family, they took the advice of Maggie's mother and called a priest. After listening to their story, beginning with the Ouija board séance in the cemetery, Father Galtier agreed to come over the next day and perform a house blessing. At first, all was quiet, much to Alec and Maggie's chagrin. They had been hoping that something unusual would happen while the priest was in the house so he wouldn't think they were making things up. As it turned out, they didn't have to wait long.

After splashing holy water in all the downstairs rooms and reciting ritual prayers, Father Galtier climbed the stairs to the second floor, the Millers following close behind. Suddenly the stench of rotting meat descended on them, along with a chilling drop in temperature. Just then, Alec spotted the shadow man ducking into Susan's room. Father Galtier walked carefully to the doorway and saw for himself the lurking figure move from behind Susan's bed to her closet, where it disappeared inside.

Turning to the Millers, the priest explained that stronger measures were now needed. He ushered them downstairs, where he had them drink holy water and recite prayers of deliverance. The house blessing had now become an exorcism. As the family prayed, noises from the upper level became louder and more absurd. It sounded like someone was dragging heavy furniture across the floor. The noises settled into a rhythmic banging, at which point Father Galtier went back upstairs alone. The racket continued, punctuated by the calm but stern voice of the priest commanding any and all evil entities to leave. After what seemed like an eternity to the Millers, a deafening boom rang out, like a loud crack of thunder, after which all was quiet.

Father Galtier came downstairs moments later, visibly shaken but still steadfast in his mission.

"Where is the spirit board?" he asked.

Maggie retrieved the garbage bag in which she had thrown the Ouija board and handed it to the priest. He took the board and planchette out, placed them on a towel, and doused them with holy water while reciting more prayers. The Millers watched in disbelief as the planchette actually lurched forward an inch with every sprinkle of the water. When he was finished, Father Galtier folded the towel over the objects, wrapped it tightly with duct tape, and instructed Alec to bury it in the far end of their yard. He told the Millers he believed their house was clean of evil spirits now, but they must never use a Ouija board again.

* * *

Years later, in an interview with paranormal investigators Greg Newkirk and Dana Matthews, Susan stated that despite the exorcism, things were never "quite right" in the house afterward. Nothing happened that was as scary as "the week with the Ouija board," but every so often something unexplainable would occur. Including the shadow man, who has been sighted by family members several times over the years. But instead of finding him frightening, now the family just accepts him. Her parents even gave him a nickname: 'Ole Charlie.

As to the mystery of the strange phrase the Ouija board spelled out that night in the cemetery—BLACK HEN—it is interesting to note that black hens were often used in witchcraft. There is actually an Italian curse called the "Spell of the Black Hen." In this ritual, hair from the intended victim is used to create an effigy of a black hen, which is then buried and left to rot. As the "hen" rots, so will the target of the curse waste away to an early death. Given that the woods near the cemetery the Millers were in were rumored to be a hotspot for black magic rituals, it's not too difficult to imagine a nefarious connection.

* * *

"There is the word GOOD BYE on every Ouija board and it is there for a very important reason. It is to close the "gate." If you do not close the board, you open yourself to just about anything that wants to come through. This is not good, and there have been some very nasty outcomes as a result."

– Christopher Ree, Global Psychics

6

Grandma's Hobby

When Ashley was 15, her grandfather died of cancer in the house he had shared with Ashley's grandmother for over 40 years. While it was a traumatizing experience for the family, they were comforted for several years afterward by what they believed was Grandpa's lingering spirit, which made itself known by the smell of roses and baby lotion. Ashley used to rub baby lotion on her grandfather's feet in his last days. And roses, his favorite flower, were always present on his bedside stand. Ashley's grandmother, in particular, was gladdened by these "visits," but when they started to occur less frequently after a few years, Ashley noticed that her grandmother began to change—and not in a good way.

Because she lived with her grandma, Ashley could see her personality change on a daily basis. Normally kind-hearted and soft-spoken, her grandmother now was becoming sullen, snippy, and *mean*. She displayed revulsion whenever Ashley's grandfather's name was mentioned, and on one occasion she loudly declared she was glad he was dead. She made cruel remarks about Ashley's appearance and actions, and often used language that would make a sailor blush. As upsetting as all of this was to Ashley, it was her grandmother's new pastime that was even more disturbing.

In her younger years, Ashley's grandmother had dabbled with witchcraft but had given it up when, according to Ashley's mother, "terrible things" had happened. But now she was throwing herself back into it with an intensity that bordered on obsession. She bought all manner of Wiccan and New Age paraphernalia: spell books, candles, amulets, pentagrams, crystals, herbs, Tarot cards, voodoo dolls, and even strange clothing like black cloaks and gowns. When Ashley asked about these things with obvious concern in her voice, her grandmother simply laughed and assured her that her little "hobby" was all just for fun.

One night when Ashley was feeling depressed over a multitude of problems going on in her life, her grandmother came over to where she was sitting and started conversing with her. Surprised but happy that her grandmother was acting normal, Ashley welcomed the older woman's support and words of advice. Then her grandmother asked her if she would like to do a meditation exercise to feel better. Ashley agreed and watched as her grandmother lit a row of small candles on the table in front of them and started up a meditation music disc on the CD player. She told Ashley to pick a candle, one that "calls to her," and focus on its flame while "willing" a spirit to control its energy. Ashley's attention was immediately drawn to a candle in the middle. As she stared intently at its flame, she felt herself gradually losing all sense of time and place. She wanted to look away but found that she couldn't. She was paralyzed, and worse, the flame was changing. It was becoming bigger, taller, brighter. What had started as a gentle, swaying light was now a frantic inferno that was threatening to engulf her. Ashley used all her mental will to break her focus from it and sharply turned her head away, at which point the flame swooshed up near her face, barely missing her tender skin.

Ashley's grandmother jumped back, a horrified expression on her face. She made brief eye contact with Ashley before blowing out the candles, all of which now were flickering calmly in their holders. "What was that?" Ashley demanded. But her grandmother only muttered something about having to check the air filter in the garage and quickly left the room. Ashley knew the incident would not be spoken of again.

Things only got worse after that. Ashley never again experienced the scent of baby lotion and roses in the house. In fact, any trace of her grandfather's comforting presence seemed to have vanished, replaced by a more disturbing, negative presence, one that Ashley felt was constantly watching her. She would frequently be awakened at night by scratching and rapping sounds within her bedroom walls. Whispered voices and unembodied footsteps made her question her sanity, while sudden drops in temperature just moving from one end of a room to another made her question her very world. She tried talking to her grandmother about these things, but only received hostile responses that were often peppered with foul language. By this point, Ashley was seriously considering moving out.

One morning while the question of whether to stay or leave was still on Ashley's mind, her grandmother came into the kitchen and said one of the dogs must have bitten her in the night. She showed Ashley two thin puncture wounds on her arm which were covered with dried blood. Ashley had seen dog bites before and she was certain that this injury was not from a dog. More disturbing were the four fresh-looking scratches, each about five to six inches in length, further up her grandmother's arm. "I don't know where those came from," her grandmother said, mystified. Ashley remembered getting up for a drink of water in the middle of the night and seeing her grandmother asleep on the couch in the living room. Everything seemed normal except for the bitter cold in the room. She had covered her grandmother up with a blanket before going back to bed and was pretty sure her grandmother's arm was injury-free at that time. She also noticed that their dogs were sleeping in a different room, where they still were when Ashley woke up several hours later.

Together with everything else strange going on in the house, Ashley had little doubt the "bite" marks were further evidence that not just a negative entity was in the house, but that a vicious, even evil, one had invaded their lives. She made a plea to her grandmother once again to give up her witchcraft and occult dabblings, and to look into cleansing the house of evil spirits. When she was done making her case, she expected her grandmother to wave off her concerns as she had done in the past, or fly off the handle and angrily ridicule her for her wild imagination.

Instead, Ashley's grandmother looked at her attentively and said, "Come with me. I have something to show you." She led Ashley over to an alcove in the hallway where a vase of flowers and a few framed photographs were arranged on a built-in shelf. Beneath the shelf on the wall below was a painted-over board with holes poked in it that made the shape of a star. Ashley's grandmother pointed to it and asked Ashley, "What do you see?"

Having practically grown up in the house, Ashley had seen this board thousands of times but had never really given it a second thought. "It's a star," she said with a shrug.

"No, look at it again, really hard this time," insisted her grandmother. "Do you see the five points of the star? Now picture a goat's head in that star, its horns filling out the top two points." Ashley's heart started to beat faster. "It's not just a star, my dear. It's a pentagram. A satanic pentagram." Ashley could see it clearly now. She had seen images of the goat's head pentagram in her grandmother's occult books. She looked at her grandmother in bewilderment.

"I can't explain it," said her grandmother, "but last week I was reading one of my books and came to a part about the pentagram. Suddenly all I could think about was the board in the hallway and I was . . . I was *pushed* to go and rip it out of the wall."

The original goat pentagram, which first appeared in the book *La Clef de la Magie Noire* by French occultist Stanislas de Guaita, in 1897.

Ashley looked closer and now could see that the board wasn't firmly attached to the wall, little jagged pieces of plasterboard around the edges giving away its loose setting. "Go ahead, take it off," her grandmother urged. Ashley took hold of the board and pulled it away from the wall. She was surprised to see a space behind it, and inside the space two objects. She reached in and pulled them out. She felt herself turn cold as she looked at what had been hidden in that secret compartment: an old, rusted pentagram amulet and a copy of the Satanic Bible. Revulsion overcoming her, Ashley dropped the objects on the floor and raced out of the house.

After taking time to catch her breath and clear her thoughts, Ashley went back inside and confronted her grandmother about the finding. Her grandmother assured her that *she* hadn't put those things there; they must have been stashed away by previous tenants. This made sense to Ashley, as both the amulet and the book looked extremely worn with age. Nonetheless, she strongly urged her grandmother to get rid of them—and all her personal occult belongings—in an effort to cleanse the house of whatever evil was in it. To Ashley's shock, her grandmother agreed.

About a week passed with no strange occurrences, giving Ashley hope that by getting rid of the occult paraphernalia they had also gotten rid of whatever had been "haunting" them. But that, unfortunately, turned out not to be the case.

The disturbing events that had bothered them before now came back with a vengeance. It started again when Ashley's grandmother went to take a shower on one particularly cold night. Though the furnace was working fine, there was an unfathomable cold inside that chilled the women to their bones. A hot shower sounded like a great idea to Ashley too, and she waited in the kitchen for her turn. A few minutes later, her grandmother came downstairs in her robe, her hair tied up in a towel. She was trying to talk, but her words came out hoarse and broken. She finally managed to say that something had tightened around her throat, strangling her. It was all she could do to break away before she couldn't breathe anymore. Ashley looked on in shock at the red imprints on her grandmother's throat. Imprints that looked exactly like fingerprints. She begged her grandmother to leave the house immediately, but her grandmother said that was going too far. She may have given up her witchcraft things, but she wasn't going to let anyone or anything make her move out of her own home.

Ashley made plans the next day to move back with her parents, but circumstances required her to stay at her grandmother's for one more week. It proved to be a hellish experience. Her grandmother's personality took on an even more sour and dark tone. The strange noises, whispering, and footsteps that Ashley had heard before in the house now were intensified and accompanied by sudden gusts of cold air and gut-wrenching whiffs of rotten smells. The doorbell would ring at all hours of the night, and lights would turn on and off by themselves. But of more concern were the physical assaults. Though they couldn't remember anything specific happening, both women woke up on multiple mornings with unexplainable bruising on their arms and legs. One morning in the shower, Ashley was aghast to see red welts on the left side of her torso.

The end of the week couldn't have come any sooner for Ashley. As she was leaving, she begged her grandmother one more time to leave also, or at least to have the house cleansed by clergy. But she got the answer she expected. A bitter, vitriolic *no*. Ashley left and never came back. Her dealings with her grandmother after that were very infrequent and impersonal.

While she tries to live a positive life now, she still harbors resentment toward the "force" that slipped into her grandmother's life and led her down such a dark path. She also remains a little angry at her grandmother for allowing it to happen. But mostly she just feels sad that the once-close relationship she had with her grandmother has been permanently damaged. As she has observed no change in her grandmother's demeanor on those few occasions that she sees her anymore, Ashley assumes her grandmother will remain a willing prisoner in that house until she dies.

That period in her life left Ashley with many unanswered questions, but there is one certainty she came away with and will never forget: once given an invitation, evil will come—and it always, *always* overstays its welcome.

* * *

> "*The infestation is usually a result of some kind of invitation, either by the current residents or a previous one, or from a curse or spell cast by a practitioner of black magic. The goal of the infestation is to increase awareness of the spirit, increase interaction with it, and finally start to control the life of the victim, or victims. Once some amount of relationship is formed and additional free rights have been given, the infestation turns mean, violent, and controlling.*"
>
> **– Adam Blai, demonologist and exorcism expert**

7

The Magic Mirror

Arlen Penzler was a disagreeable, spiteful middle-aged man who lived alone in central Pennsylvania. Arlen had no close friends, couldn't stand to be around family members, and blanched at the thought of hanging out with co-workers after office hours. Traditional sports and hobbies didn't interest him, as he had always considered himself above the pedestrian pursuits of common people. No, Arlen was convinced he was meant to pursue bigger things, secret things, empowering things. So day and night, in a quest to fulfill his destiny, Arlen devoted himself to his one true passion: the occult.

After Arlen's grandmother passed away and left to him a five-foot-tall ornate antique mirror, he became particularly interested in a branch of the occult called mirror magic, an ancient practice that witches and black magicians utilized to foretell, and even manipulate, future events. The more Arlen studied mirror magic, the more convinced he became that this was the *big thing* he had been waiting for. This would give him what he so deeply craved: power over others.

When he felt he was finally ready to try it out for himself, Arlen placed the mirror before him and performed a lengthy incantation ritual that involved, in part, invoking spirits to do his bidding. Then he peered into the mirror as one would a crystal ball, focusing all his attention and will on it while awaiting a picture of things to come. After a lot of sweat and a headache from a half-hour of intense concentration, Arlen was disappointed that all he saw were blurry and fleeting images that meant nothing to him. But it was a start.

As the days and weeks went on, and as his concentration became stronger, the more clearly Arlen was able to see things in the mirror. Eventually he gained control over *what* he wanted to see—people, places, events—as well as *when*. A day into the future, a week, a month—Arlen now had the power to see future events whenever he chose. He was delighted. The mirror magic was working just as the ancient rites had promised.

Seeing the future was incredible, but what Arlen really wanted was to *shape* it for his own purposes. That would make him a true sorcerer. He knew exactly where he would start: with all the people who throughout his life had slighted him, made fun of him, or whom he just didn't like.

He made a list of targets and planned the ways he would exact his revenge. There was the woman from work who claimed Arlen had harassed her. *Yeah, right,* he thought. *You just wanted me fired so you could have my job. How would you like to fall down a flight of stairs, you freakin' phony?* Then there was his cousin, who at their grandmother's funeral said Arlen owed him three hundred dollars. *The stinking liar,* Arlen muttered under his breath, as he jotted down in his notebook, *"Make V's wallet disappear."* And how about that stupid pharmacist who got his prescription wrong the week before? Because of him, Arlen had to wait an extra 30 minutes at that germ-infested drugstore. *You idiot, you'll get so sick your doctor won't know what hit you.*

Arlen knew it would take a lot of effort and skill to mentally "project" his intended victims into future scenes in the mirror and then "will" misfortunes to befall them. But he was up to the challenge. Plus, all he had to do was envision it. Spirits under his command would do the dirty work of carrying out his intentions. The mere thought of performing this magic made Arlen downright giddy. He had been studying the occult for most of his life, and never did he imagine he could wield so much power. With the spirit world at his beck and call, the possibilities of what he could do were endless. There was just one problem.

Arlen had forgotten, or chosen to ignore, a rather important part of the original ritual—the part that gives homage to Satan. This didn't go unnoticed. As a consequence, the evil Arlen wished on others now began to boomerang back to him. The spirits he expected would terrorize his "enemies" were instead beginning to terrorize him.

Arlen found himself living in a house of horrors. Doors and drawers opened and closed by themselves. Objects levitated and were flung across the room by invisible hands. Unintelligible voices whispered behind his back. Disembodied footsteps stomped around the house.

Frightening noises echoed in the night. And black, shapeless shadows appeared in corners and entryways.

Arlen was terrified. He called the local Catholic diocese and demanded that an exorcist come out to his house. The church official he talked to explained that no priests were readily available, but that he would send Ed and Lorraine Warren out to help. Ed was a prominent and highly-respected demonologist, and his wife, Lorraine, was a light trance medium with clairvoyant abilities. The official assured Arlen that the Church had worked with them many times in the past and could testify to their effectiveness. At that point, Arlen was willing to accept anyone's help.

* * *

The Warrens drove out to Arlen's house later that same day. As soon as they stepped inside, they knew there was a big problem. Not only was Arlen visibly shaking with fear, but the house was "alive" with paranormal activity. Objects were swirling around the room and crashing into walls; doors and cupboards were flinging open and slamming closed; lights were flickering on and off. As if that wasn't enough to impress the newcomers, Ed happened to look out the window and saw his car sitting in the middle of the street, crossways and blocking traffic. A witness told Ed that the car rolled slowly out of Arlen's driveway until it came to a stop where it was now. Ed found the car with the doors locked and the parking brake set, just as he had left it in the driveway.

While the inside (and outside) of the house had more shenanigans going on than a three-ring circus, the Warrens found the situation to be no laughing matter. The "clowns of hell" had to go before someone was seriously injured in either body, soul, or both. The most direct way of ending the demonic siege was to reverse the spell that Arlen had performed, or, as Ed called it, "stabbing the devil with his own pitchfork."

Ed conducted the reversal successfully, which put an immediate end to the spirit activity. Arlen's enthusiasm for "commanding" demons did a quick reversal itself, and he begged the Warrens to take the mirror away with them, which they did and which to this day hangs in the Warren's Occult Museum in Connecticut. Getting the mirror to its new home, however, was a terrifying challenge in itself.

With the mirror safely stashed away in the trunk of their car, the Warrens started back on their long drive home. From past experience, Ed knew that the malicious spirits attached to the mirror could very well make him the new target of their wrath. With that in mind, he made a conscious effort to drive very carefully. About five miles from Arlen's house, the car hit a small pothole, certainly not big enough to inflict damage under normal circumstances. But this evening, the circumstances were anything but normal. A new radial tire exploded, causing the Warrens to veer dangerously into oncoming traffic. As Ed later reflected, it was a miracle they weren't killed on the spot.

After Ed was able to pull over and change the tire, they ventured forth again. Before long a large tractor-trailer—

notably missing any lettering, design, or plates, Ed noticed—pulled into the lane ahead of them. Though the pavement was bone dry, the truck suddenly started kicking up green, gummy sludge that splattered across the Warrens' windshield, temporarily blinding them. The windshield wipers were barely able to cut through the slime, but when it finally lessened, Ed and Lorraine were astonished to see that the truck had disappeared. But not for long. Minutes later it came up behind them again, passed them on the left, veered back to the right in front of them, and again let loose with the green goo. When he could see again, Ed was not entirely surprised that the truck had again vanished from sight. The green slime game happened several more times before Ed was able to exit off the parkway onto a less-busy road leading home.

After about an hour of driving on the back road with no incidents, the Warrens were feeling like they just might make it home in one piece after all. That is, until Ed looked in the rear-view mirror and spotted a black car racing up behind him at breakneck speed. Though it was now dark outside, the car had on only its parking lights, giving it a sinister, predatory-like look. Oblivious to the icy conditions, the black speedster passed the Warrens on the left, missing them by mere inches.

As Ed watched the car disappear down the road, he couldn't shake the feeling that something wasn't right. A moment later his instincts were proven true. Ed had just maneuvered their car onto a one-line suspension bridge when he watched in disbelief as the black car turned around at the top of the hill and began careening toward them at what had to be 90 miles per hour. The Warrens were frozen with fear. They wouldn't make it off the bridge before the crazed driver plowed right into them. They said a prayer to St. Michael and braced themselves for what they surely believed was their end.

But then the incredible happened.

Instead of crashing into the Warrens head on, the black car passed *through* them. *A phantom*, Ed realized with relief. It had been a phantom car all along. Shaken but feeling blessed to be alive, the Warrens made it home without experiencing any other paranormal disturbances.

As for Arlen's magic mirror, it is safely ensconced in the Warrens' Occult Museum, its power nullified by a binding ritual and blessing. Visitors to the museum are encouraged to look around as much as they like, but are also warned not to touch any of the objects. It might be a good idea to not gaze too long into any mirrors, either. You might not like what you see.

* * *

Divination by means of mirrors has several names: catoptromancy, crystallomancy, and scrying. The practice has been around in different forms since ancient times and recently has received a renewed interest by some members of the psychic community, who believe mirrors can increase their clairvoyant abilities.

Many occultists use mirror magic for communicating with the spirits of the dead, navigating the astral plane, exploring past lives, and affecting healings. While these are more or less "positive" uses for mirrors, there are other uses—as we've just seen—that are less than admirable. In particular, summoning a spirit and "trapping" it within a mirror can prove disastrous, especially if the mirror is given or sold to a new owner with the spirit still inside. Already angry over its imprisonment, the spirit is likely to cause as much trouble as it can for its new owner.

Other problems can arise when dabbling with mirror magic, such as "opening" a wrong door, or forgetting to "close" a door, and then having to deal with uninvited and unwanted visitors. Sometimes a mirror will start out as "just a mirror," but becomes "active" when paranormal activity ensues around it, as in the case of haunted houses.

"The spirit world is right beside us, but we don't see it most of the time. Mirrors twist the psychic space and provide openings," says paranormal expert John Zaffis. So should we be worried about the mirrors we have in our houses? Probably not. Be a little careful, though, about bringing a second-hand mirror into your home. Find out who the previous owner was. Pay attention to any bad vibes you feel from it. Trusting your gut is often the first line of defense against paranormal disturbances. Mirrors in bedrooms can also be problematic. Zaffis recommends not having mirrors situated in a bedroom where a person can see himself or herself in bed. And definitely don't place a mirror above the bed. Another piece of advice: mirrors should never reflect into each other, even from different rooms. "This configuration seems to widen the opening between dimensions," Zaffis explains.

Mirror, mirror, on the wall . . . is that a demon come to call?

8

The Dream House

Since the time she was a little girl, Pam had experienced a recurring dream about living in an old colonial farmhouse in New England. Why she had this dream had always been a mystery to her, as she was born and raised in Ohio and as an adult lived in New Mexico. She had no roots at all in New England. Yet the dreams were so vivid that over the years she started entertaining the idea of actually moving to the East Coast, especially if the "house of her dreams" should ever become available.

In the meantime, Pam shared an apartment in Albuquerque with her best friend, Barbara, while continuing to eke out a living in retail. The work was not satisfying, though, and the pay was poor. Additionally, Pam began suffering bouts of depression and at one point even contemplated suicide. It seemed to her that no matter what she did, happiness, contentment, and financial security remained elusive, and therefore so did the life she had always imagined for herself.

Desperate for a change of affairs, Pam turned to the dark arts for help. She bought a book on witchcraft and performed a prosperity spell. She figured she had nothing to lose and everything to gain at that point. And gain she did. About two months after performing the ritual, Pam secured a prestigious, high-paying job. Her worries, for a while at least, were put to rest.

But there was still something nagging at Pam in a deep corner of her mind: the farmhouse from her dreams. Her finances now in a healthy state, Pam began monitoring the real estate ads in New England area newspapers. After about two years of obsessive searching, she finally found a listing for an old farmhouse that seemed almost too perfect to be true. Convincing her roommate to accompany her, Pam and Barbara drove out east and took their first look at the house on January 1, 1977. To Pam, the rural house set back in a wooded area a mile from the main road was indeed perfect. But it would take a total of three trips to the house over the next year before she was ready to commit to it.

Finally, in December of 1977, Pam quit her job and started making arrangements to buy the farmhouse. She and Barbara had agreed they would start a new, simpler life out east and dedicate themselves to raising animals within the beautiful confines of nature. But an unexpected glitch came up when the bank announced that although Pam had more than enough cash for a sizable down payment, it needed three signatures on the mortgage. While this formality was annoying to Pam, it wasn't a deal-breaker, as her sister Vicky agreed to co-sign the loan along with Pam and Barbara.

The deal now done, Pam and Barbara went back to their apartment that night elated that their lives were about to change. What they didn't know at that point, and had no reason to suspect, was that their lives were indeed going to change, but not in the positive way they were anticipating. A portentous sign of their future came to them that very night.

After bidding each other good night, the two women retired to their respective bedrooms. Just as they were drifting off to sleep, they were suddenly jarred to full consciousness by the sound of heavy footsteps in their apartment. This was followed by loud pounding on both of their bedroom doors. Terrified but unable to reach the phone, which was out by the "intruder," the women spent a horrifying night listening to the on-again, off-again sounds of heavy walking and raps on their doors, which interestingly always came in groups of three.

At some point during the night, Pam and Barbara eventually fell asleep. When they ventured out of their rooms in the morning, they couldn't believe what they saw. Nothing. There was no indication that anyone had been in their apartment; moreover, the deadbolt was still in place on the door, as undisturbed as it had been when the women locked up the night before. Understandably, Pam and Barbara were extremely eager at this point to leave New Mexico.

At the end of January 1978, the women completed their move to the New England farmhouse. But instead of finding a peaceful, idyllic life in the country, Pam and Barbara experienced further discord and disturbances. In fact, the very first day they arrived at the farm they felt as if they were being watched by an invisible presence. As the days went on, the two women tried to focus on fixing up the house but found themselves bickering with each other over every little thing instead of accomplishing any work. The atmosphere in the house didn't just affect the women either. Their two dogs, normally even-tempered and friendly, started barking incessantly and attacking each other, so much so that they had to be kept in separate parts of the house. Making things worse, the feeling of being watched intensified to the point that on several occasions Pam and Barbara opted to spend the night in a nearby motel.

Soon it was more than emotions and feelings being affected by the house. Unexplainable physical incidents began to take place. As the women tried to continue their renovations, their cleaning products would disappear and in their place would be drops of blood. Money, combs, and other small objects would vanish, never to be found again. At night, they frequently heard ominous chanting from outside the house. One afternoon at around 3 p.m., they heard knocks on the back door. No one was there. When the women went out to investigate, they saw footprints leading from the door to the barn. But only *left* footprints. And so shallow in the powder-soft snow as to have been made by something no heavier than a cardboard cutout.

After a few months, Pam convinced her sister to come out for a while to help with the restoration projects. But Vicky was an extremely sensitive young woman who herself had been dealing with emotional issues, and as soon as she walked into the farmhouse, a wave of terror washed over her. She was so upset that she apologized to Pam, turned right around and left for home. Unfortunately, Vicky's terror didn't end at the farmhouse. Several days later, she tried to commit suicide by stabbing herself with a butcher knife. The doctors were amazed that she survived what should have been mortal wounds—three of them, in fact.

Not long after Vicky's short-lived visit to the farm, Barbara decided she too could no longer stand the repulsive and oppressive feeling of evil that permeated the estate. Despite her strong misgivings to not leave Pam alone, she nonetheless moved out and returned to the town in Ohio where she once lived. But like Vicky, Barbara didn't leave unscathed. Not more than a few days after settling into a new apartment, Barbara was viciously raped by an unknown intruder. Though logic dictated that it was just a coincidence, Barbara knew that her attack was somehow connected to the New England house and that if she didn't return, she would suffer even greater physical consequences. Despairingly, she moved back to the farmhouse.

Life for Pam and Barbara continued to get worse over the next several months. Unnerving noises, objects moving or disappearing, shadowy figures seen from the corners of their eyes—all of these things and more haunted their days and nights at the farmhouse. But worst of all were the changes being made to the women themselves. Physically, they seemed to be aging at twice the normal rate. Their skin developed deep and numerous wrinkles. Their hair turned from brown to gray. Their faces sagged and their eyes became hollow. Their appearances alarmed some of the local townspeople who did occasional business with the women. But though Pam and Barbara knew what was happening to them, they were too afraid to leave their house, their "prison," for fear of even worse punishments.

Changes overtook the women's personalities as well. Bickering was now replaced by all-out fits of anger, shouting, and violent remonstrations. The worst episode came when Pam rented a chainsaw to cut down a tree that blocked a front window. Just as she was about to put the first nick in the trunk, Barbara came racing out, screaming at the top of her lungs. But it was her appearance that truly frightened Pam. Barbara's face looked nothing like the Barbara she knew, even when upset. It was *altered*. It was the face of someone else, someone who was not just angry, but truly evil. Raging maniacally, Barbara threatened to kill her if she so much as touched the tree. That was the turning point for Pam, the moment she will always remember as the "awakening" to the metaphysical evil that had invaded their lives.

Not knowing who to turn to, but knowing she needed help, Pam began making inquiries around town. Her story about living in a haunted house and being terrorized by evil spirits was met with plenty of skepticism. One person even jokingly suggested she go to nearby Salem, where maybe she could find a "good witch" to take care of things. Finally, she made the decision to call the local Catholic church. As the daughter of a Baptist minister, Pam had an inbred suspicion of Catholicism, but at this point, she was willing to try anything. Father Michael Ryan met with her that same day, listened to her story from beginning to end, and then gave her a surprising response.

"I know that house. It has a very dark history. I'm surprised you weren't told of it before moving in." He then went on to explain that years ago it was rumored that the house was used by a group of Satanists who performed profane rituals on the property, including animal sacrifices. Pam stiffened when she heard this. She recalled the strange behavior of her dogs, the eerie sounds of chanting in the middle of the night, and the overwhelming atmosphere of sorrow that permeated the inside and outside of the house. She asked what she should do. Move out, he advised. But first, he strongly recommended she and Barbara see him in person for a special blessing, a "minor exorcism" that would help break the hold the demonic had seemingly placed on them.

Pam and Barbara put the farmhouse up for sale later that week. Then they met with Father Ryan and discussed with him in more detail the events of their lives over the past couple of years. As more details emerged, Father Ryan had no doubt the women had been battling demonic oppression. In addition to the major events that took place, including the still-distorted features on the women's faces, many seemingly minor things occurred that were characteristic of the demonic: things happening in groups of three, disturbances at 3:00 o'clock, only *left* footprints appearing.

The priest then asked if they had ever engaged in any occult activities before coming out to the farmhouse. Pam sheepishly admitted she had performed a witchcraft spell for prosperity a few years back. Father Ryan nodded and told them that could very well have been the opening the demonic used to "groom" Pam for her move out east. It obviously already knew about her farmhouse dream—it may even have planted that seed. Once it had her on its hook with the illusion of her dream come true, it was just a matter of time before it broke down her mind, spirit, and body to the point of insanity, possession, or death.

Luckily, Pam and Barbara escaped from their hellish farmhouse before the most dire consequences could beset them. After receiving the priest's blessing, they returned to New Mexico, where they continued their lives with a keener perception of all things visible and invisible. Pam was particularly wary of giving too much attention to her dreams after that point. She would never allow herself to forget how the house of her dreams became the house of her nightmares.

* * *

Along with dabblers and practitioners of the dark arts, there are also innocent bystanders who somehow get snared by the occult. Like tragic victims of a drive-by shooting, they are simply in the wrong place at the wrong time. They might buy their dream house or move into a nice little apartment, not suspecting the horror that awaits them."

– Ralph Sarchie, demonology expert and former NYPD Sergeant

9

The Witches' Hex

In the following case, the victim did nothing of his own initiative to invite evil into his life. He first started feeling its presence as a small boy, then on and off throughout his young adult years. According to many exorcists, this is not unusual. Evil spirits can, and do, target all sorts of people. They are looking for a way in. They are looking for acquiescence. Real problems—diabolic obsession, oppression, and possession—start to arise when the target gives in, either through continual, non-repentant acts of immorality (sin, in religious parlance) or through dealings with the occult.

In Peter's case as described here, it was the latter reason his troubles escalated. He knew the women he chose to hang out with one winter night were witches but chose not to care. Because of that choice, he opened the door to the ever-patient demons that had been knocking for so long. Peter's story should serve as a warning to all of us that even slight brushes with the occult can have devastating consequences.

* * *

Peter's first direct encounter with evil happened when he was 10 years old. He was awoken from a light slumber around midnight when the radio turned on by itself.

"The lunatic is in the hall."

Peter was paralyzed with fright. Though he couldn't see anyone in the room with him, he knew someone, or something, was there. A presence. A bad presence. He tried to thrash around and cry out but could do nothing. Nothing except lie helplessly in his bed while the presence in his room grew stronger and the words from the radio became more ominous.

"There's someone in my head, but it's not me."

* * *

Peter's life would continue to be plagued with episodes like this. "I'd have a feeling of something scary being present. Then something weird would happen," recounts Peter in an interview with *Crisis Magazine*.

One such incident happened when Peter was visiting home during a college break. He was awakened at 1:30 a.m. by a strong feeling that someone was approaching the front door of the house. He went downstairs just as his sister came staggering through the entryway. He followed her into the living room and began talking to her about the dangers of drinking too much. Suddenly he was overcome with that familiar feeling that someone or something else had just entered the room. Something dark, threatening, and frightening. The phone rang and Peter just about jumped out of his skin. He answered it and a woman's voice said, "Don't even try to talk to her. Just leave her alone." Peter hung up, shaken, but still determined to talk some sense into his sister. Then the phone rang again. This time the woman's voice was distorted, like she had rocks in her mouth. "I told you not to talk to her!" the voice demanded. Peter stopped his lecture after that and went back to bed.

Peter's parents, being religious people and open to the possibility of supernatural occurrences, had always believed the stories their son told them, and they believed him now. They arranged for him to meet with a clergyman, who explained that some people are simply more attuned to the preternatural world. They sense things better, things that remain hidden to most other people. Things like demons.

Peter learned to live with his "condition" grudgingly, holding out hope that someday, either through the grace of God or boredom on the demons' parts, he would be left alone. Unfortunately, not only was the preternatural world not yet bored with Peter, it was soon to unfold its biggest attack thus far.

Peter was 20 and at home on winter break. After a frustrating experience at a church meeting in which he got into an argument with another member, Peter went to his friend Janelle Gobel's house, hoping to take her to a movie. Peter and Janelle had been friends since elementary school. The Gobels were an all-female household consisting of Janelle, her two sisters, and their mother. Peter had never asked about Janelle's father, nor did he know where the Gobel's got their money. As far as he knew, Janelle's mother didn't work, yet the family appeared very well-to-do.

One thing Peter did know was that the Gobels had more than a passing interest in the occult. He had seen books on witchcraft and other esoteric subjects lying around the house on prior visits. When he asked once what religion, if any, they practiced, Mrs. Gobel replied that they were more interested in studying their ancestry than practicing any conventional religion, and cited as points of interest the Old Testament accounts of animal sacrifices and scapegoats. Peter remembered nodding politely while suspecting that Mrs. Gobel—and probably her daughters—were witches of some sort. But because he really liked Janelle, he told himself he could overlook their peculiarities. After all, didn't his own religion teach tolerance?

When Peter arrived at Janelle's house that winter evening, Mrs. Gobel greeted him warmly and insisted he sit down and wait while she finished baking. Soon Janelle and her sisters joined him, chatting amiably for 20 minutes until their mother came out with a plate of cookies. Peter helped himself, wondering briefly why he was the only one eating. And why weren't the cookies warm? Before he could wonder too much, Mrs. Gobel grabbed his attention with a strange spiel about Moses actually being a woman, having horns, and other "weird stuff." Then she put her hands in front of her face, palms facing out, and intoned, "All of sudden you open your eyes and you see what's going on."

Peter was transfixed. Mrs. Gobel kept talking, but Peter had stopped hearing the words. He was disoriented and confused. Were the cookies drugged?

Suddenly Janelle's voice broke through his reverie. She announced it was time to leave and she would drive. Glad to get away from Mrs. Gobel, Peter got in the car and was once again surprised when instead of going to the movies they arrived at an old, abandoned house about ten miles away. Still in a bit of a haze, he docilely let Janelle lead him inside where they sat and waited—for what Peter didn't know. After a short time, Mrs. Gobel and Janelle's sisters arrived. Mrs. Gobel approached Peter and said, "He's ready to meet you downstairs if you want."

From some deep recess of his mind, Peter was able to gather enough clarity to answer firmly, "No!" Somehow he knew that the "he" waiting downstairs was not someone he wanted to meet. Mrs. Gobel received Peter's answer calmly and began making small talk with her daughters, as if sitting in a spooky dark house was the most natural thing in the world. During the idle chit chat, Mrs. Gobel repeated her invitation several more times. *"He's ready to meet you downstairs if you want, Peter."* And each time Peter answered with a *no*.

They finally left the house and told Peter they were taking him to a movie. But to this day Peter remembers nothing of where they went and little of the movie itself. In fact, he only remembers one scene, one in which a goat's neck was slit open and people were dancing around the butchered animal and the flowing blood.

Afterward, in the car, Janelle laughingly asked Peter if he enjoyed "the part about the goat." Then her tone changed and she announced that they were going back to "that house." Something snapped in Peter, and he had a sudden inspiration to not just ask to go home but to demand it. "Janelle, take me home!"

"No," Janelle answered. Peter repeated his order, even more emphatically.

Janelle became flustered, and she turned and asked her sister Rebecca what to do. Rebecca told her she has to do whatever Peter says. The women drove him back to his house without another word and left him there for the culmination of what would be the worst night of his life.

* * *

Peter's sister, Carolyn, was still up when he returned home. She remembers that he was acting and talking strangely. She could tell he wasn't drunk—there was no hint of liquor on his breath and he wasn't slurring his words—but he definitely wasn't himself. She wondered about drugs, but that was so unlike Peter as to be unbelievable. He told her he was going back to the church community he had been at earlier that night. Then he said a final-sounding goodbye and left.

In spite of his altered condition, Peter somehow made it to the church. He doesn't remember much of the drive other than being scared silly at the cars whizzing by him. It was late when he arrived. Pounding on the door, he woke the priest and laypeople who lived there and frantically stated that he believed God wanted him to live there too. The priest calmly explained that God doesn't inspire vocations through fear. Then he left briefly and returned with a fresh set of clothes. Peter had wet his pants.

After he changed, Peter sat in a chair and stared at a crucifix on the wall. Some of the men in the community were watching nearby and could tell Peter was growing more agitated by the minute. Suddenly he shouted, "Forget God!," and jumped up and ran down the hall to the chapel, pushing three men out of his way. Then, in front of gaping witnesses, Peter stood on a pew and did a perfect backflip. Someone yelled to call the police. Peter then raced toward the sanctuary, breaking several statues along the way. He was tackled and held down by six men. Peter broke free and continued his rush toward the front of the chapel. He later related that he was intent on getting to the tabernacle. He wanted nothing more than to crawl right inside it. He needed God so badly, he remembers.

The police soon arrived, put Peter in a straitjacket, and threw him into the back of a police van. "That was the deepest, worst psychological thing I'd ever experienced. It was so heinous and evil," he recalls. At one point, he thought that maybe he was actually in hell. The police brought him to a psychiatric ward, where he remained under evaluation for a week before getting a clean bill of mental health.

Peter's life, for the most part, went back to normal after that night with the Gobels. But what was normal for Peter was not, of course, normal for most people. Strange things continued to happen around him. His sister, Carolyn, had a job at the time answering phones for a security company. The work was very boring—except when Peter called to chat. Unfailingly, when he called on her personal line, she would receive calls on the security lines. Weird calls—eerie laughter on the other end, voices speaking in foreign languages or in complete gibberish, disturbing noises she couldn't identify. Peter finally quit calling her at work.

One day months after the back-flip incident, Peter was out walking with a friend when a grotesque-looking old woman with blank eyes came up to him and said in a deep male voice, "I have a message for you." She then smiled at him and urinated right there on the ground. Peter was immediately reminded of his own "accident" that night in the chapel.

Several years later, after many more incidents like these, Peter's brother arranged for an exorcism. He brought Peter to a priest, who performed a simple exorcism under the auspices of a casual conversation. Not wanting to alarm Peter or conjure up unwanted dark thoughts, the priest asked Peter a few questions and did a few tests, never once saying the words "exorcism" or "devil." Then, making it appear like a mere afterthought, the priest said some prayers over Peter, some in English, some in Latin, and sent him cheerfully on his way.

It would be nice to say that Peter lived happily ever after following the exorcism, but unfortunately, that hasn't been the case. He is still tormented, still hounded. An exorcist in the diocese of Denver, Father Herman Jayachandra, reviewed the details of Peter's case and doesn't think that Peter was ever possessed. A possessed person would not have run toward something sacred like a tabernacle. He would have run away from it. He would not be able to use holy water or go to church or pray without great difficulty, all things that Peter continues to do.

Father Herman believes that Peter is being oppressed by a demon. Oppression is one step down from possession and is often characterized as an unrelenting external attack by an evil spirit whose intention is to wear the victim down and cause discouragement and despair. The demon hates its victim and will go to great lengths to keep that person entrenched in the misery of self-doubt about their sanity. And like bedbugs and lice, rarely do demons make easy or clean departures. They hang around for months, years sometimes, never letting their victims rest, never letting them forget.

Father Herman further believes that Peter's oppression is most likely the result of witchcraft, something he had seen a lot of during his years of ministry in India. Undoubtedly that night at the Gobels' house unleashed a far greater evil force into Peter's life than what had been there previously. And since he had known Janelle Gobels from the time he was ten years old—the age when strange and disturbing events started happening in his life—it's very probable he had been hexed to a lesser degree even earlier.

Peter's sister has stated that most people who know Peter don't see anything wrong with him. But inside, he suffers greatly. He wavers between hope and despair, and he is often angry at God for allowing this tribulation in his life. Which is exactly what his tormentor wants. As author Tom Hoopes puts it, "The devil is an oppressive, energy-draining weight on the spirits of those afflicted by him. He isn't into artful repartee, he doesn't play the fiddle, and he can't make you a rock star. He won't keep his promises. And he hates you beyond imagination."

* * *

"The devil, after using a witch to the best interest of both, eventually will kill her indirectly, driving her mad so she'll die quickly in an accident or slowly from not being able to care for herself."

– Fr. Herman Jayachandra, Diocese of Denver

10

Cupid Comes Calling

The breakup hit Max harder than he could ever have imagined. For one thing, it came out of the blue. One minute he and Lisa were sharing a tender, candlelit dinner; the next she was telling him she had met someone else. He recently had been considering proposing to Lisa, and now she was dumping him like yesterday's leftovers. They parted ways that night after making awkward promises to remain friends. But as weeks, and then months, dragged by, Max knew he could never think of Lisa as just his friend.

Unlike most spurned lovers who eventually succumb to time's healing powers, Max continued to obsess over Lisa. He called her once after the breakup, but Lisa made it clear she was not interested in getting back together. A few months later, Max heard through friends that Lisa was getting married to the guy she had chosen over him. This news made Max's already-inflamed jealousy rise to new heights. He worked even harder to figure out a way to win Lisa back. Finally, he thought of something that on the surface seemed ridiculous, but maybe, just maybe, had the potential of being incredibly effective. Magic.

Why not? Max thought. He wasn't getting anywhere by natural means. So why not try supernatural means? What if he could put a spell on Lisa that made her choose Max over her new husband? It was worth a shot, Max decided. He took a trip to the local occult bookstore and bought an armful of books on magic, spells, and witchcraft. When he got home he pored over them and soon decided that while, yes, there were plenty of spells and rituals he could perform that might do the trick, they were a bit more complicated than he expected. He needed the help of a professional.

He made an appointment with a local white witch, Gabriella, who advertised the casting of love spells, among her many other services. When Max went to see her, he showed her a picture of Lisa. "Can you help me win her back?" he asked. Gabriella asked for more background on his and Lisa's relationship and the circumstances of their breakup. When Max explained that Lisa had recently married, Gabriella immediately gave him his photo back and told him she found true love for people; she did not break up marriages.

Discouraged, Max went back home and considered his next move. He would do the spell himself, he decided, by making something personal for Lisa and embedding a spell within it. Remembering that Lisa loved cherubs, Max found a picture of a cherub that he thought Lisa would like and set about rendering his own version of it in black and white. While he worked, he recited the words to a love spell he had composed himself and mentally transferred his thoughts of Lisa into the drawing. He looked at his finished creation with a sense of elation and hope. Lisa would love it, he had no doubt. Now he just had to get her to accept it.

When Lisa received Max's phone invitation for lunch, she wanted to beg off, but Max's good-natured insistence persuaded her to accept. It was just two friends getting together for lunch to catch up, she told herself. When she met Max at the restaurant, she carefully avoided any overture of affection and quickly sat down across from him. As they talked about what was going on in their lives, Lisa got the distinct impression that Max was acting as if nothing had ever changed between them. *He's acting like we're still a couple*, she marveled. After dessert and their last cup of coffee, Lisa started plotting her exit. Their lunch had dragged out too long, as far as she was concerned. But then Max surprised her by pulling out a flat gift-wrapped package. It was a late wedding present, he explained. Lisa graciously, if not somewhat awkwardly, accepted it and, at Max's nudging, opened it right there. Her shock was not something she had to fake.

"I knew you'd like it," Max enthused. "I drew it myself, to make it more personal. Who knew I could draw, right?"

Lisa gulped. "Who knew, indeed." While on the outside Lisa was trying to maintain a polite demeanor, inside she was trying to hold down her lunch. The picture was hideous. Was Max being serious in thinking that she'd love it? Not only could a five-year-old draw a better angel, this one seemed intentionally *demented*. Its eyes were coal-black little circles and its mouth was shaped into a smirk. There was absolutely nothing cherubic about this cherub. Nonetheless, Lisa thanked Max for the present and departed quickly. For some reason she felt colder than usual.

After arriving at home, Lisa showed the picture to her husband, Ethan, who made no attempt to hide his disdain. "That's the ugliest angel I've ever seen," he said. Lisa agreed and then assured Ethan that even though Max seemed to still have feelings for her, she bore none for him. Eager to get the disturbing drawing out of sight, she then brought it down to the basement and stashed it on top of some old boxes. Out of sight, out of mind.

But while the cherub may have been out of Lisa's mind, Max for some reason wasn't. In the days that followed their lunch, Lisa found herself thinking of Max more and more. And, surprisingly, in a fond way. She replayed their recent lunch date over and over in her mind while thinking about how kind and thoughtful Max had been. She reminisced about the good times they had shared in their relationship. She even had erotic dreams of him at night. One day a few weeks after their lunch, Lisa was rummaging around in her jewelry drawer and came across some pieces Max had given her when they had been dating. Though she hadn't thought about that jewelry for years—in fact, she was still surprised she had any of it—she felt compelled to start wearing it. Ethan was not pleased.

"Are you still seeing him?" Ethan demanded to know.

"Don't be silly! Of course not!" But though she knew the jewelry upset Ethan, Lisa couldn't resist wearing it. This led to several fights between the couple. And soon they were fighting over every little thing.

During their verbal spats, the tension in the house seemed to grow exponentially and inanimate objects suddenly seemed to come to life. Dishes rolled off counters, pictures dropped from their hooks, and on one occasion a vase fell off a shelf all on its own and crashed to the ground. In bed at night, Lisa frequently heard sounds of footsteps in the house and would spend many anxious hours cowering under the blankets, as Ethan refused to be bothered.

Lisa suspected that their house had become haunted somehow, and reached out to a friend for help. That friend put Lisa in touch with paranormal investigator John Zaffis. John met with Lisa and Ethan at their home and began asking questions not just about the strange occurrences taking place in the house, but also about more mundane, human events taking place in their lives. John knew that spirit activity often was drawn to personal turmoil and dysfunctional relationships. And it was quickly apparent that the relationship between Lisa and Ethan was strained. When John probed a bit in that regard, Ethan angrily told him to ask Lisa about the jewelry she was wearing—Max's jewelry.

It was true, Lisa admitted sheepishly. She was wearing jewelry given to her by an old boyfriend. But for the life of her, she didn't know why. Her hand went to the strand of pearls around her neck. She had no feelings for him anymore, she said as she looked at Ethan pleadingly, but for whatever reason she couldn't get him out of her mind.

"And this *obsession* just started recently?" asked John.

Lisa nodded. "About three months ago. Right after I had lunch with him and he gave me that god-awful drawing."

John's suspicions were immediately alerted. "What drawing is that?"

"It's supposed to be a cherub, but it looks more like a grotesque little goblin. Max was proud of having drawn it himself. He said it was a belated wedding present."

John asked to see the picture. He immediately saw what Lisa meant about it being grotesque. He was also pretty sure its repulsiveness was more than surface deep.

"Was Max into the occult that you knew of?" John asked Lisa.

"I, I don't know—"

John told her he suspected Max had put a spell on her via the drawing.

"A spell?" Lisa was shocked.

What most likely happened, he explained, is that Max channeled a love spell into the picture, probably while he was drawing it, which then transferred to Lisa when she accepted it. Unfortunately, a negative spirit (or two or three) apparently came along for the ride.

Lisa had heard enough. After John performed a cleansing and binding ritual to break the spell, she asked him to take the picture away. Then she went through her jewelry and threw out all of the pieces that had come from Max. As John had told her, any inanimate object that has or had an emotional connection to someone can serve as a link for paranormal activity given the right circumstances. Lisa was taking no chances.

Finally, she called Max and confronted him about the spell. He confessed, saying he had been desperate to win her back after hearing that she was about to get married. He was sorry, he told her, not only for the trouble it had caused in her life but also because things weren't going right in his, either, since making that drawing. He couldn't shake a feeling of gloom and doom that had settled on him. And making matters worse, he hadn't gotten a good night's sleep for weeks due to strange noises in the house. He agreed not to bother her again, wished her well, and hung up.

Max's troubles weren't surprising to John. "I have seen some forced love spells that have a temporary effect, and the person who does the spell thinks they are going to get what they want. In the end, they lose. Something always goes wrong. The spells can still cause a lot of trouble until they backfire."

Since getting rid of the creepy cherub, Lisa's life has returned to normal. She feels like her old self again, the strange disturbances in the house have ceased, and she and Ethan have gotten their relationship back on track.

The cherub still exists, safely ensconced in John Zaffis' Museum of the Paranormal, powerless in general but still sending chills up the spines of onlookers with its soul-piercing, beady black eyes, and its not-so-angelic leering smile.

* * *

"In love situations, unless you have the permission of the person on whom the spell is cast, you are doing something against their free will. This has serious karmic repercussions . . . It is the use of magic for purposes to serve our own needs. It could even be called "black magic" — the use of universal forces for evil. You may get what you want, but you will pay dearly for it karmically."

– Sataya, The Love Psychic

11

Charlie Charlie

In the spring of 2015, it topped nearly every social media chart and was one of the most heavily Googled terms: Charlie Charlie. Although not new in essence, this newly-branded spirit invocation game was going viral among teenagers all across the globe. Anyone could do it. No expensive supplies were needed and no arcane knowledge was required. All you needed were two pencils and a piece of paper. Players were urged to record their game sessions and post them online under #CharlieCharlieChallenge. By the end of May, that hashtag had been tweeted over 2 million times, and to this date is still going strong.

So, what exactly is Charlie Charlie?

Basically, it's a Ouija board-type game where players draw two intersecting lines on a piece of paper resulting in four quadrants. The words "yes" and "no" are written in alternating quadrants. Two pencils are then placed crosswise on top of each other in the center so they are lined up with each axis.

Now the player asks the question: "Charlie, Charlie, are you here?" If the Charlie spirit (rumored to be a Mexican demon) is present, it will move the top pencil to a "yes" quadrant. The player can then go on to ask other questions of it.

"It" is what has drawn concerns from parents, teachers, clergy, and even doctors. What is this spirit named Charlie, and is it real or just an easily-induced imaginative figure that can nonetheless still cause physical and mental harm?

Skeptics are quick to point out that the tenuous positioning of the pencils makes them susceptible to movement by the slightest vibration or breath of air. Furthermore, they argue, the game suspiciously started trending right before the release of the Hollywood movie *The Gallows,* suggesting it was a marketing stunt. And finally, there is no Mexican demon named Charlie.

All of the above is true. But to those who believe the game is a true occult venture into the netherworld of demons, none of that matters. It's not the mechanics or the media attention or the misnamed evil entity that counts. It's the intent of the players that matters. The players are invoking a demon to "play with." It doesn't matter if they use pencils and paper, or feathers and parchment, or a letter board with a plastic planchette. If the invitation is made, the guests will come.

And when they do, it isn't always for fun and games.

Mackenzie Cussler from Chelmsford, England reported that when she tried out the challenge, nothing happened at first. But then about five minutes later she heard a distant scream. Right after that, the mirror in her room cracked for no apparent reason. Terrified, she ran into her sister's room where a bookshelf tumbled over by itself.

Julie Loftus from Syracuse, New York, had an even spookier experience. She asked Charlie, "Am I going to die tonight?" When the pencil moved to "yes," Julie admitted she was a little freaked out. She tried to shrug it off and went to the kitchen to do the dishes. But soon she heard noises coming from her room. She went back and found her bible lying on the floor face down. At first she thought the cat must have knocked it over but then remembered that the cat was spending the night at the vet's office. When she heard whispering coming from right outside her room, she slammed her door, locked it, and called her mom to come over and spend the night with her.

Hank Correti's experience was a bit more intense. Playing the game in his hometown of Jacksonville, Florida, Hank taunted Charlie by saying, "You're fake, you're not real. Come and get me if you're here!" Suddenly Hank was pushed face down and violently attacked. He recounted that it felt like someone was cutting him with razor blades. After the attack stopped, Hank's friends saw that his back was covered in scratch marks.

In a letter to his students at a Catholic high school in Philadelphia during the height of the Charlie Charlie Challenge craze, Father Steven McCarthy warned, "I want to remind you all there is no such thing as 'innocently playing with demons.' The problem with opening yourself up to demonic activity is that it opens a window of possibilities which is not easily closed. Please be sure to NOT participate and encourage others to avoid participation as well."

Cody Miller from Texas gave the same warning after his own terrifying experience with Charlie Charlie. "Do not attempt to do this challenge!" he posted on his social media outlets. This came after he and some friends did the challenge in a shed in Cody's backyard. Cody reported that while no questions were answered during the game, he felt an uneasy presence and a burning sensation on his hand, back, and lower leg. The boys ended the game quickly and walked back to the house, but to their surprise they couldn't get in because all the doors were locked. Cody knew he left the doors open since they were only going 50 feet away. Luckily, he had his keys on him and they went inside.

As soon as they entered the house, they all experienced a deep foreboding, as if something evil was there watching them. Trying their best to shrug it off, the boys sat in the living room and turned on the TV while one of them, Rob, went into the kitchen for a drink. A minute later they heard a scream. Cody ran in and found his friend babbling hysterically about seeing "something" in the cupboard. Cody looked but saw nothing but the usual glasses and plates. He guided Rob out toward the living room, and that's when he saw his own horrific vision: an unmistakable man figure at the top of the stairs with black and red eyes. Cody and his friends fled from the house and stayed away until Cody's parents came home from work. Nothing more out of the ordinary occurred. And, of course, no more Charlie Charlie was played.

Amy Todd from Derbyshire, England, was playing Charlie Charlie one night with some friends when suddenly the power went out in her house. Amy asked Charlie "and any other spirits present" to turn on her laptop which was sitting idly nearby with its lid up. Instantly the laptop screen lit up, inducing screams and jumps from the players. After a few minutes, the other lights in the house came back on. With her heart still racing, Amy asked Charlie if it would now leave them alone. The pencil moved to "no." Amy's friends had had enough. They said goodbye to Charlie and any other present spirits and urged Amy to come to one of their houses for the night. Amy looked over at Simon, her large German Shepherd who was lying down near the hallway, and, acting braver than she felt, told her friends she'd be fine. After all, the game was over.

Twenty minutes later, all of Amy's lights went out again. Not only was it unusual for that particular neighborhood to experience power outages at all, to say nothing of twice in one night, but when she looked out her window, Amy saw that all of her neighbors' lights were still on. She started to call her parents on her cell phone to see if they were having the same problem when her phone inexplicably died. At that same instant she heard Simon start to growl. That was enough. Amy grabbed her purse, called Simon to her side, and raced out the front door. She stayed with a friend that night, and the next morning arranged for a minister to perform a "cleansing" of her house. She reported no further disturbances after that.

The exact origin of Charlie Charlie is a bit fuzzy, but it appears to be a modern incarnation of an old Spanish game called *Juego de la Lapicera* (game of the pens). Popular in Spain as well as parts of Central and South America, Lapicera has been played by generations of school-age kids, particularly girls who are eager to know which boys in their class "like them." The current version was first publicized in April 2015 by a local TV news report in the Dominican Republic about an alarming "satanic" game overtaking local schools. Social media users immediately came on board and soon the phrase "Charlie Charlie" was inundating Twitter, Instagram, and Vine, first in the Dominican Republic and soon after throughout the Spanish-language Web. From there it was a mere puddle jump to the rest of the world.

And, indeed, the world took notice. In Jamaica, the Ministry of Education issued a ban on playing the game. The Fiji Ministry of Education did the same. In Italy, a middle school in the province of Verona prohibited the game to avoid upsetting sensitive students. Several elementary and high schools in Cape Town, South Africa, also banned the game and threatened to expel any student caught playing it. One principal stated: "I have a good school and I don't tolerate these kind of disruptions."

The most dramatic report to date of menace and mayhem caused by Charlie Charlie hails from the Choco region of Colombia, where on July 9, 2016, twenty-two schoolgirls between the ages of 12 and 15 displayed symptoms of mass hysteria, including convulsions, hallucinations, fainting, and paranoia after playing the Charlie Charlie game. The children, who were playing the game in a number of separate classrooms, were brought to a hospital by their teachers where video footage showed several girls writhing on the ground, screaming, and even foaming at the mouth. One girl stated that she saw a man dressed in black who threatened to kill them all.

Medical tests were conducted that ruled out disease, intoxication, the use of hallucinogenic substances, or any other underlying health conditions. After a while, the girls' vital signs returned to normal and they were released to the care of their parents. Claudia Patricia Asprilla, the mother of one of the involved girls, said her daughter "doesn't want to go to school because she's afraid, she's frightened, and last night she started to get scared again. I'm worried about this because this is a scary thing. It's something you can't explain." Caracol News reported afterward that local authorities were visiting the affected girls' homes, offering psychological, social, and spiritual help.

Spanish exorcist Fr. Jose Antonio Fortea weighed in on the Charlie Charlie Challenge in an interview on May 27,

2015. In no uncertain terms, he described the dangers of "calling on spirits." He warned that "some spirits who are at the root of that practice will harass some of those who play the game." Even though the priest thinks that players won't necessarily be possessed, the spirit that has been invoked "will stay around for a while." Fr. Fortea further warned that playing Charlie Charlie, or similar "games" such as the Ouija board, "will result in other spirits beginning to enter into even more frequent communication. And so then the person really can suffer much worse consequences from the demons."

Or djinns.

It's not just the Christian community that has taken issue with Charlie Charlie. During the height of the frenzy in 2015, the Islamic community in Jamaica issued a condemnation of the game: "It should be taken very seriously, as it may release demonic elements (djinn) . . ." Dr. Sulaiman Tijani, youth adviser at the Islamic Council of Jamaica, explained, "In the djinn world, there are good and bad or evil. However, the djinn that is summoned in this game, if the reports are true, would be [one of the] djinns that are not good. ... Look at the results where children have to be hospitalized for psychiatric and behavioral strains." When people play the game, Tijani stated, they "are actually summoning this djinn, and when you summon the djinn, what happens to the child is the end result."

Whether it's demons, djinns, or a spirit named Charlie being summoned, or whether it's simply a demonstration of physics in action and people's imaginations running wild, the Charlie Charlie Challenge is probably best left to dwell in the dark regions of cyberspace, where it all began in the first place.

* * *

"The Evil One is smart. He knows how to entice people with seemingly harmless things ... I have dealt with too many situations involving people who, perhaps innocently, started dabbling in the occult. They now wish they could go back and undo their prior decision."

– Fr. Stephen Doktorczyk, Diocese of Orange, California

12

The Demon Ritual

Martin Friedman's life-changing encounter with evil came after a slow descent into the occult that started when he was a young man and continued for many years after. His story is meaningful because it dramatically shows how innocent curiosity in the arcane can very often lead to participation in the profane. Often with disastrous results.

* * *

In 1956, Martin was born into a middle-class Jewish family in New York. His parents weren't overly religious, but did keep the customs and traditions of their faith and educated their children likewise. Martin attended Hebrew school where he learned to read, write, and speak Hebrew, and at age 13 he celebrated his bar mitzvah.

But three years later an incident at his synagogue made him lose faith in his religion. It was Rosh Hashanah, the Jewish New Year, and attendance at the temple service required the purchase of a ticket, as was customary for the High Holidays. Martin had his and was waiting for things to begin when he saw an elderly woman looking for a chair in the crowded space. Seeing no empty seats, Martin got up and offered her his. Immediately an usher came over and told him he couldn't do that. The old woman did not have a ticket and therefore was not entitled to a seat, the usher explained. Martin looked at him dumbfounded, then laughed and walked out. He never again set foot in any synagogue.

When he was 17, Martin had his first experience with the occult when his friend took him to an occult shop in town that was owned by the friend's cousin. Martin was impressed by the friendliness and knowledge of the shop owner and was intrigued by the vast collection of books and wares on display and for sale. The shop owner introduced him to a pair of regular customers, Jane and Steven, who were practicing Wiccans. They talked to Martin at length about their beliefs and invited him to a "pagan circle" where he could learn more. Martin was hooked and spent the next several months with his new friends learning about pagan deities, Wiccan rituals, and of course, spells and magick. They called themselves "white Wiccans," and always made it clear to themselves and others that they intended no harm to anyone with their rituals. Soon Martin was a full-fledged practitioner of "The Craft."

After high school, Martin joined the Air Force. To his delight, he discovered that there were Wiccan groups and covens all over the country, so no matter where he was stationed, he could practice his craft with others. He also discovered through his travels that Wicca was just one aspect of witchcraft; there were much darker components of the occult web, as he was soon to find out.

It was a beautiful summer day in San Francisco when a man walked up to Martin in a shopping mall. He was carrying a red leather satchel with an inverted pentagram emblazoned on it. Martin's curiosity was piqued. He was familiar, of course, with the pentagram. His Wiccan groups used them all the time, but theirs were not inverted. The man introduced himself as a member of the First Church of Satan and invited Martin to one of their ceremonies. While Martin had no interest in (knowingly) worshipping Satan, he was interested in seeing how this group differed from his own. He agreed to go.

What Martin ended up attending was a black mass. When he arrived, he was told to remain in his seat and quietly observe, no matter what happened. What followed was a vile and blasphemous parody of the Eucharistic celebration practiced by the Catholic Church. The officiant of the "mass" was a defrocked priest, the altar servers were nude women, and the bread and wine used in the ceremony had been stolen from a local Catholic church. As the "priest" did disgusting things with the communion wafers and the wine, all under the shadow of a massive inverted crucifix, Martin sat in his seat transfixed. He was horrified at what he was watching, and though he wanted nothing more than to flee as far as he could from this place of hatred and filth, he physically couldn't. Some unseen force held him in his chair as securely as a vice.

When it was all over and he was allowed to leave, Martin couldn't stop thinking about the terrible scene he had just witnessed. He kept assuring himself that Wicca was nothing like that. Wiccans didn't even believe in Satan. Obviously, whatever "power" those demented individuals thought they were invoking via their sick ritual was all in their heads. And though they tried to get into his as well, Martin was having none of it. His nature-based pagan path was life-affirming, peaceful, and positive. The world just made more sense when viewed through a Wiccan lens. Or so Martin told himself.

Several years after the black mass incident, and following his discharge from the Air Force, Martin became the high priest of a coven near his home. One day he was paid a visit by his old "mentor," Steven, who had kept up his own Wiccan activities through the years but was now delving into darker aspects of the occult and wanted Martin's help. Steven wanted to conjure up a demon. He told Martin he had been studying from authentic occult ritual books and was confident he could do it. It would be easier, though, with a partner, and it would be nice to have a witness if successful. In spite of his uncomfortable memories of San Francisco, Martin agreed to help out. After all, he didn't really believe in the devil anyway, so what harm could come of it?

A few nights later, they met at Steven's house and began performing the demon-raising ritual as described in a much-revered book of ceremonial magick. Steven assured Martin that as long as they stayed within the lines of the protective circle inscribed on the floor, they would be safe no matter what. By this time, Martin was beginning to feel uneasy. The atmosphere in the room had changed; it was heavy and ominous. There was "something" there with them, Martin was sure of it. Flashbacks to the satanic mass flooded his mind. He had felt the same way back then.

Suddenly, from out of nowhere, a beautiful woman materialized outside of the circle. Voluptuous and enticing, she beckoned Martin to come over to her. Martin was too terrified to breathe, let alone move. As he stood there, his heart and mind racing but his feet frozen to the floor, the woman slowly changed into her true form—the most hideous creature Martin had ever seen or imagined. A nauseating stench rolled off the beast in waves, and when it took a step toward him, he thought for sure he would collapse and die on the spot. But then the creature disappeared, as instantly and mysteriously as it came. Relief washed over Martin, and he could see by glancing over at Steven that his friend was breathing easier too. But their relief was short-lived.

The wall they were facing started to shake and gradually dematerialize, replaced by a vision of what Martin later stated was a "glimpse of hell." Shrouded in shadows and smoke, the scene before them unfolded like a nightmarish play. Far-off screaming and cursing echoed up from somewhere deep below, while a ghoulish collage of human and demonic faces floated through the haze. If the stench from the first vision was horrible, it was now a hundredfold worse. Sulfur, rotten eggs, decaying flesh—no words could describe the foul odor that blanketed the room.

Then the demon came. A shadow at first, it steadily grew in stature and clarity until its full terrifying form stood before the two men a mere arm's length away. Martin's sanity began to crumble, as the sight before him was too horrifying for his mind to comprehend. It wasn't just what he was seeing—although that was hideous beyond belief—but what he was *feeling* from this grotesque beast: a hatred, so pure and evil that it made Martin want to die to escape it. The demon turned to Steven, laughed and said, "Do you really think this circle can stop me?" Then it picked Steven up and threw him across the room into a wall fifteen feet away. Martin's reverie was broken. He ran out of the room to the back of the house and locked himself in a bathroom.

How long he stayed there Martin can't remember. But he knew after some time had passed that he had to check on Steven. He cracked the bathroom door and listened. He heard no screaming or cursing. He detected no foul smell. He slowly made his way back to the ritual room, and as he approached he thought he could hear Steven talking. When he entered the room, his heart dropped. His friend was slumped against the wall, foaming at the mouth, and babbling incoherently. Steven's glazed eyes told Martin all he needed to know. His friend wasn't dead, but he was gone all the same. Martin called the police and told them he had dropped by and found Steven in this state. He was pretty sure the police wouldn't have bought a story about a demon attacking them.

Steven never did recover. He spent the next 20 years in a psychiatric institution where he eventually took his own life. Though Martin escaped physically unscathed, emotionally and intellectually he was forever changed. He had stared evil incarnate in the face and had seen the devastation that can occur by challenging it. Unsatisfied with Wicca's notion that evil is not a thing but only a word to describe actions, Martin decided to leave Wicca for good.

On a freezing February day, he called together members of his coven and some other coven leaders to tell them of his decision. Things got ugly fast. Words were exchanged, pushing and shoving ensued, and finally, punches were thrown. Martin stormed out of the house and sat in his car waiting for the old heap's engine to warm up enough to drive away. As he waited, several of the men he had been fighting with came outside and began walking toward him. Although Martin couldn't hear them, he could tell by the synchronized movement of their mouths that they were chanting an invocation. Within seconds he was proven right, when without warning the driver's and front passenger's side windows blew out. Martin threw the car in drive and sped off, not once looking back.

Only when he was a safe distance away did it dawn on him that there was no glass inside the car. The windows had blown out, not in. Once again, he had come away from an encounter with evil without so much as a scratch. At that moment, Martin considered the idea that if evil was a real and tangible thing, then it stood to reason that its opposite must be also. There was good just as there was evil, and for reasons he couldn't begin to understand, it seemed to be protecting him.

Martin spent the next two decades searching for the Source of good that he felt had protected him during his dark years in the occult. He drifted in and out of various Christian denominations before finally being baptized in the Catholic Church. He has made his story known to warn people away from the occult—all parts of it. While some strands may appear harmless, they're all part of the same dark and dangerous web. Once a spider is alerted to something in its trap, it's only a matter of time before it comes for its prey.

* * *

"There are two equal and opposite errors into which our race can fall about the devils. One is to disbelieve in their existence. The other is to believe, and to feel an excessive and unhealthy interest in them. They themselves are equally pleased by both errors and hail a materialist or a magician with the same delight."

– C.S. Lewis

Closing Thoughts

There is a seductiveness to the occult that ensnares many people with its promise of an easy path to knowledge, wealth, and power. It preys in particular on those who are already beset in life with misfortunes such as sickness, depression, and bankruptcy, offering magical cures for all that ails them. It also sends its siren call to those with less-than-admirable character traits, such as excessive pride, greed, lust, and cruelty. What better circus to join than one that doesn't judge and condemn, but only wants to aid and abet?

The problem comes later when the main act is over and the ringmasters decide to tear it all down. You see, demons lie. They tell partial truths only when it helps them manipulate and scheme their way toward destroying people, families, and institutions. This pattern of hate-fueled treachery has been revealed time and time again through the rite of exorcism, when demons are compelled to speak the truth. That is why they will try so hard to remain hidden, and why in the early stages of occult activity, a practitioner won't suspect that anything is wrong. Unfortunately, once the practitioner does realize that something is amiss, it's often too late.

Evil is a reality, and as these accounts have shown, there are consequences to opening up doorways that invite it into our lives. While this book *is* intended to scare you away from the occult, it is *not* intended to make you despair. Good always wins over evil in the end. If you are unfortunate enough to experience something strange, threatening, or frightening in your life because of known or suspected occult interaction, the time to act is now. Reach out to those who can help you. Remove all trappings of the occult from your home. Renounce all attachment to the occult from your psyche. Then walk away as fast and as far as you can.

Better yet, don't get involved in the first place.

Selected References

Amorth, Gabriele. *An Exorcist: More Stories*. Ignatius Press, 2016.

Bagans, Zak. *I am Haunted: Living Life Through the Dead*. Victory Belt Publishing, 2015.

Blai, Adam. *Possession, Exorcism, and Hauntings*. CreateSpace Independent Publishing, 2014.

Brittle, Gerald. *The Demonologist: The Extraordinary Career of Ed and Lorraine Warren*. Prentice-Hall, 1980.

Dewey, Caitlin, "The Complete, True Story of Charlie Charlie, the 'Demonic' Teen Game Overtaking the Internet." *Washington Post*, May 26, 2015.

Fortea, Antonio. *Interview With An Exorcist*. Ascension Press, 2006.

Guiley, Rosemary, and Philip J. Imbrogno. *The Vengeful Djinn: Unveiling the Hidden Agendas of Genies*. Llewellyn Publications, 2011.

Hoopes, Tom. "The Dark Backward: Demons in the Real World." *Crisis Magazine*, November 1, 2003.

Hundley, Tom. "Italians See Magic As a Way of Life." *Chicago Tribune*, June 7, 1997.

Martin, Malachi. *Hostage to the Devil: The Possession and Exorcism of Five Living Americans*. Reader's Digest Press, 1976.

Newkirk, Greg. "The Unfinished Boleskine House Ritual: Did Aleister Crowley Accidentally Summon the Loch Ness Monster?" *weekinweird.com*, April 11, 2011.

Newton, Michael. *Raising Hell: An Encyclopedia of Devil Worship and Satanic Crime*. New York: Avon Books, 1993.

Ray, Rachel. "Leading U.S. Exorcists Explain Huge Increase in Demand for the Rite–And Priests to Carry Them Out." *UK Telegraph*, September 26, 2016.

Sarchie, Ralph, and Lisa Collier Cool. *Beware the Night: A New York City Cop Investigates the Supernatural*. St. Martin's Paperbacks, 2001.

Torres, Hazel. "New Case of 'Mass Demonic Possession' Reported in Colombia Affecting Schoolgirls Playing 'Charlie, Charlie.'" *Christianity Today*, July 13, 2016.

Welton, Benjamin. "Image of the Beast: Parsing Aleister Crowley's History and Fantasy." *The Airship*, October 10, 2014.

Zaffis, John. *Shadows of the Dark*. iUniverse, Inc., 2004.

Zaffis, John, and Rosemary Guiley. *Haunted by the Things You Love*. Visionary Living, 2014.

About the Author

John Harker is a freelance journalist and ghostwriter who's been writing and publishing since the 1990s. His personal encounters with unexplainable phenomena have inspired him to explore strange, dark, and disturbing topics in both non-fiction and fiction. He lives with his family in eastern Washington, where the ghosts are dry and dusty.

Visit John's website, johnharkerbooks.com, for updates on new book releases and other information.

Also by John Harker

When Demons Attack: True Tales of Diabolic Encounters

Demonic Dolls: True Tales of Terrible Toys

Ouija Board Nightmares: Terrifying True Tales

Ouija Board Nightmares 2: More True Tales of Terror